Newcastle
City Council
Newcastle Libraries and Information Ser\

☎ **0845 002 0336**

Due for return	Due for return	Due for return
D22		
20/6		
17/7	2 5 JUN 201	
	16 JUL 2011	
	17 AUG. 2011	
	2 9 Mar. 12	

Please return this item to any of Newcastle's Libraries by the last
date shown above. If not requested by another customer the loan
can be renewed, you can do this by phone, post or in person.
Charges may be made for late returns.

EXPLORING THE
ISLANDS
of
ENGLAND
AND WALES

INCLUDING THE CHANNEL ISLANDS
AND THE ISLE OF MAN

A FRANCES LINCOLN BOOK

First published in the UK in 2007 by
Frances Lincoln Publishers Ltd
4 Torriano Mews
Torriano Avenue
London NW5 2RZ

A catalogue record for this book is available from
the British Library.

ISBN 978-0-7112-2743-9

Printed in Singapore

Produced for Frances Lincoln Publishers Ltd by Julian Holland

Photography and design
Julian Holland

Cartography
Stirling Surveys

Editorial
Denise Stobie

Proofreading
Linda Wright

Below *The wild and beautiful island of Bryher in the Isles of Scilly is only a 20 minute helicopter flight away from Penzance, followed by a short boat crossing from Tresco. Lashed by Atlantic storms in winter and for centuries a graveyard for unsuspecting ships, Bryher's west coast provides the perfect antidote to the stress of modern life.*

EXPLORING THE
ISLANDS
of
ENGLAND
AND WALES

INCLUDING THE CHANNEL ISLANDS
AND THE ISLE OF MAN

JULIAN HOLLAND

F
FRANCES LINCOLN LIMITED
PUBLISHERS

CONTENTS

Introduction	6	Bryher	50
		St Martin's	52
Channel Islands	8	St Michael's Mount	56
Jersey	10	Looe Island	58
Guernsey	14	Burgh Island	60
Herm	18		
Sark	20	**Southern England**	62
Alderney	22	Brownsea Island	64
		Isle of Wight	68
South West England	26	Hayling Island	76
Steep Holm	28	Thorney Island	80
Lundy Island	32	Isle of Sheppey	82
Isles of Scilly	36		
St Mary's	38	**Eastern England**	86
St Agnes and Gugh	42	Canvey Island	88
Tresco	46	Foulness Island	92

Wallasea Island	94
Northey Island	96
Mersea Island	98

Northern England	**102**
Farne Islands	104
Holy Island (Lindisfarne)	108
Isle of Walney	112

Isle of Man	**114**

Wales	**124**
Anglesey	126
Holy Island	134
Bardsey Island	136
Ramsey Island	140

Skomer Island	144
Caldey Island	148
Flat Holm	152

Index	**156**
Acknowledgements	**160**

Below *Higher Town Bay on the virtually traffic-free island of St Martin's is one of the many deserted white, sandy beaches that can be discovered on the Isles of Scilly. Here, only a short distance from the congested mainland, visitors can finally unwind and take in the breathtaking beauty that surrounds them.*

INTRODUCTION

Unknown to millions of people, many of the islands scattered around our coastline are priceless gems waiting to be discovered and explored. In an age when cheap air travel allows us to visit far-flung corners of the globe, there – right on our doorstep – are some of the most beautiful, and sometimes remote, places in the world. A short boat, plane or helicopter crossing from the mainland will take you to our little-known crown jewels, where you can unwind from the stress of modern life and take in the rich panoply of their natural beauty, wildlife and historical legacies.

A few of the islands in this book are part-time islands, only cut off from the mainland at high tide, while others are now connected to the mainland by a bridge, but each has its own unique character. For the first time this book, profusely illustrated with specially commissioned photographs, not only offers a fascinating insight into the history and natural history of many of our islands, but also offers practical advice: on how to get there, where to stay, tourist information, what to see and where to walk.

From the deserted white, sandy beaches and clear blue seas of the Isles of Scilly, the funfairs and beach huts of Hayling Island and the rugged remoteness of Lundy Island, to the Art Deco experience of Burgh Island, the teeming birdlife of the Farne Islands and Skomer Island, or just the pleasure of having a pint with the landlord of the George & Dragon pub on windswept Foulness Island – there is so much to discover out there. Enjoy it!

Above *One of the highlights of visiting our islands is the amazing diversity of birdlife that can be seen on them. On the Pembrokeshire island of Skomer, the 6,000 pairs of puffin attract thousands of human visitors between June and August each year.*

Below *Each of our islands is a microcosm of our country's historical past. Here, overlooking L'Ancresse Bay on the Channel Island of Guernsey, Martello Tower No. 4 stands testimony to past wars between England and France.*

THE CHANNEL ISLANDS

JERSEY
GUERNSEY
HERM
SARK
ALDERNEY

Left *This massive concrete German naval artillery direction and range-finding tower, known as MP3, on the northeast coast of Alderney is a grim reminder of the Occupation of the Channel Islands during World War II. Beyond is the lighthouse on Quenard Point. Built in 1912, it guides ships through the treacherous stretch of water known as Alderney Race, between the island and mainland France.*

Jersey

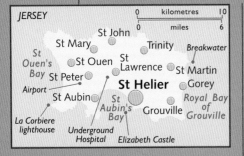

O nce home to hunters and gatherers of the Early Stone Age and later ruled by the Dukes of Normandy, the island of Jersey became a possession of the English Crown in 1204. Along with the rest of the Channel Islands, Jersey was for centuries in the front line of European conflict. Peace only finally settled on the island in 1945 with the surrender of German occupying forces. With customs and traditions that date back to Norman times, the 90,000 people of the Bailiwick of Jersey today enjoy their status as a self-governing British Crown dependency. Aided by a mild climate and low taxation regime, the traditional industries of agriculture and tourism now sit comfortably alongside modern electronic commerce, offshore banking and financial services as Jersey's main economic activities.

Below *Founded in 1878, the Royal Jersey Golf Course overlooks the Royal Bay of Grouville on Jersey's east coast. Taken with the bay's beauty, Queen Victoria gave it the royal title after a visit to the island in 1846. In the distance Mont Orgueil Castle, built in the 13th century, stands in a commanding position overlooking the bay and the village and harbour at Gorey.*

HISTORY

Stone artefacts discovered in a cave on the southwest coast of Jersey show that the island was occupied thousands of years ago by Early Stone Age man, when it was still physically connected to the French mainland. The cave, La Cotte de St Brelade, is one of the most important Palæolithic sites in the whole of Europe. The first farmers arrived on Jersey about 7,000 years ago, leaving behind a rich legacy of their ancient religious rituals and burial rites. The most important site from this period is the burial chamber at La Hougue Bie, to the northeast of St Helier. The Romans certainly used the Channel Islands as a staging post between France and England but, apart from the remains of a possible temple at Pinnacle Rock in the northwest of the island, few remains from this period have been found on Jersey. During the 6th century, St Helier brought Christianity to Jersey, living and preaching from the rocky outcrop in St Aubin's Bay known as the Hermitage. By the early 9th century Jersey, along with neighbouring northern France, had come under attack from Viking raiders.

By the 10th century, the Vikings had taken control of what was to become the Duchy of Normandy and, in 933AD, Jersey and the rest of the Channel Islands were incorporated into the Duchy. Many of the customs, laws and traditions of Jersey date back to this period of feudal rule. Following the Norman conquest of England by William the Conqueror in 1066, the Channel Islands came under the control of the English crown. In

Right At four miles long, St Ouen's Bay is the longest stretch of sandy beach in the Channel Islands. Popular with surfers and fringed by dunes, its gently curving arc stretches from La Pulente in the southwest to Etacquerel in the northwest. Perched on a rocky outcrop in the distance, La Rocco Tower was one of 31 coastal towers built at the end of the 18th century to defend Jersey against French attack.

1204, when King John of England lost his Norman lands, the people of the Channel Islands chose to stay loyal to the English crown and sever all ties with nearby France. This switch of allegiance brought about nearly 600 years of both threatened and actual attack from France.

To defend Jersey against attack, many fortifications were built around the island. The first, Mont Orgueil Castle at Gorey, was built during the 13th century to defend the island's east coast. This was breached in 1461 when French troops seized the island and held it for seven years. By the end of the 16th century Elizabeth Castle, named after the then reigning Queen, was built on a rocky outcrop in St Aubin's Bay to defend the expanding town and harbour of St Helier.

From 1778, war with France again threatened Jersey, and the many Martello towers that were built during this period can be seen all around the island's coastline today. The only actual landing by French forces occurred in 1781, when troops led by Baron de Rullecourt marched on St Helier and forced the Lieutenant-Governor of Jersey to surrender. However, troops from the English garrison led by a young officer, Major Peirson, attacked and defeated the invaders. Following the defeat of France in 1815, peace finally settled on the island and its economy boomed. Boatbuilding, agriculture, cattle rearing, cider making, stone quarrying and oyster farming all thrived throughout the rest of the 19th century and into the 20th. During this period, Jersey's tourist industry, assisted by its mild climate, improved sea links with England and royal patronage, also grew from strength to strength.

All of this peace and prosperity abruptly came to end at the outbreak of World War II. Deemed by Churchill as undefendable, Jersey and the rest of the Channel Islands were invaded by German forces in the summer of 1940. Lasting five years, the Occupation brought about great deprivation and, towards the end, near starvation for the people of Jersey. Thousands of slave labourers from Nazi occupied Europe were brought to the island to build massive concrete defences and underground tunnels. Peace finally returned to Jersey when the German forces surrendered without a shot being fired on 9 May 1945.

Since the end of World War II, Jersey's economy has boomed again and, today, assisted by its status as a self-governing British Crown dependency outside of the European Union and low taxation regime, agriculture and tourism take their place alongside financial service industries and electronic commerce as the island's chief economical activities.

THE JERSEY RAILWAY

One of two former railway lines on Jersey, the Jersey Railway opened between St Helier and St Aubin in 1870. The railway was built to the British standard gauge but later converted to 3ft 6in gauge when it was extended to Corbière. Plans to electrify the seven-mile-long line in 1906 did not materialise, and the railway closed for good in 1936. Today, the former terminus building at St Aubin (right) is now a police station and the trackbed of the railway line between St Aubin and Corbière has been converted to a cycle way and footpath. The second railway on Jersey, the Jersey Eastern Railway, ran from St Helier to Gorey and was opened in 1872. However, increasing competition from buses led to its closure in 1929.

NATURAL HISTORY

The largest of the Channel Islands, Jersey contains a wide variety of natural habitats. Its 50 miles of coastline includes the magnificent St Ouen's Bay in the west, with its four miles of sandy beach and large areas of dune and heathland. Together with the headlands at each end and the large freshwater St Ouen's Pond, much of this western coastal strip is now protected for the enormous variety of plant and wildlife that is found within it.

With its steep cliffs and coves, Jersey's rugged north coast is home to large numbers of seabirds during the breeding season. During spring and early summer, the coastal footpath winds its way through colourful carpets of wildflowers.

In the southeast corner of the island,

Right *A World War II German observation post stands like a menacing sentinel overlooking Corbière lighthouse on Jersey's southwestern corner. Completed in 1874, the lighthouse can be reached along a causeway at low tide.*

the vast intertidal area exposed at low tide is rich in marine life and, during winter, is an important feeding ground for thousands of wading birds.

Jersey's coastal wetland areas are so important that four of them - the South East Coast, Les Ecrehous and Les Dirouilles in the northeast, Les Pierres de Lecq in the northwest and the offshore islands of Les Minquiers - are all designated Ramsar Wetland Sites. A fifth, St Ouen's Bay and Les Mielles, has also been proposed.

Inland, the reservoirs at Queen's Valley in the east and Vale de la Mare in the west provide an important habitat for freshwater birds. Wooded valleys, such as the protected St Catherine's Wood in the northeast, are also a favourite haunt for Jersey's red squirrel population.

Finally, Jersey is the headquarters of the world famous Durrell Wildlife

Conservation Trust, founded by the pioneering naturalist and author Gerald Durrell in 1959. Formerly known as Jersey Zoo, Durrell Wildlife is located four miles north of St Helier in the Parish of Trinity.

HOW TO GET THERE

By air There are direct flights to Jersey from many airports in the UK and from Guernsey, Alderney and a selection of European airports.

By sea Condor Ferries operate a regular high-speed catamaran service to Jersey from Weymouth, Poole, Portsmouth, Guernsey and St Malo. For more details contact their reservations office (tel. 0870 243 5140) or visit their website: www.condorferries.com

Manche Iles Express operate a high speed catamaran service to Jersey from Granville on the Cherbourg peninsula. For more details visit their website: www.manche-iles-express.com

TOURIST INFORMATION

Jersey Tourist Information Centre, Liberation Square, St Helier, Jersey JE1 1BB (tel. 01534 500777) or visit their website: www.jersey.com

WHERE TO STAY

Jersey offers a wide variety of accommodation, from hotels and guesthouses to self-catering units and campsites. For details contact the Jersey Tourist Information Centre (see above).

ISLAND WALKS

A series of footpaths offers good coastal walking, from La Pulente in the southwest along the less populated west and north coasts to Rozel in the northeast. There are also footpaths following the coastline of the Portelet peninsula from St Aubin to St Brelades. The island also has a network of Green Lanes, where priority is given to walkers and cyclists and the speed limit for vehicles is 15mph.

PLACES TO VISIT

● Corbière Lighthouse
● Jersey Museum, St Helier
● Maritime Museum, St Helier
● Fort Regent, St Helier
● Elizabeth Castle, St Helier
● Jersey Zoo
● German Underground Hospital
● La Hougue Bie Museum, Grouville
● Pallot Steam Museum
● Grosnez Castle
● Mount Orgueil Castle, Gorey
● Samares Manor

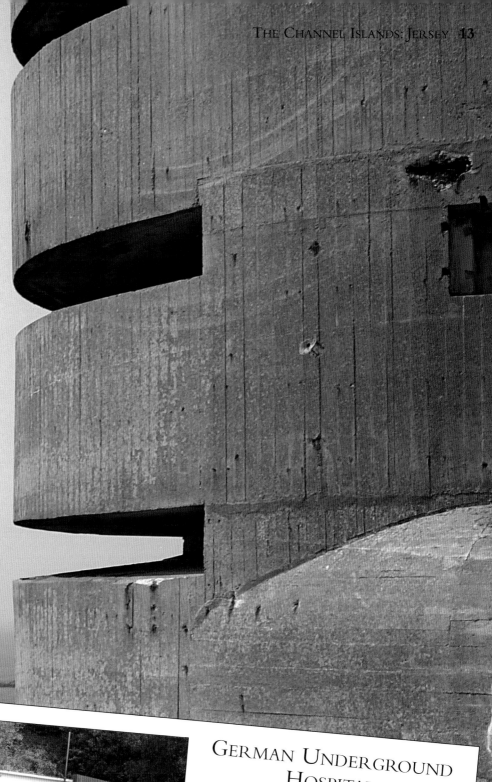

GERMAN UNDERGROUND HOSPITAL

During the German occupation of Jersey in World War II, hundreds of slave labourers from many European countries were forced to work in appalling conditions to create this complex of tunnels in St Peter's Valley. Hewn out of solid rock and known as *Ho 8*, it was originally intended to shelter the island's entire German garrison from attack and provide storage for ammunition, vehicles, fuel and food. Never completed for its original purpose, the complex was converted into a military hospital during 1944. In its final guise, it contained an operating theatre and wards for 500 casualties. The expected Allied invasion never came and the Germans surrendered on 9 May 1945. The complex has since been restored and is open to the public.

GUERNSEY

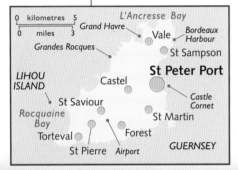

With a population of over 65,000, Guernsey is the most densely populated of the Channel Islands. Occupied by man for the last 7,000 years and an important trading post during Roman times, the island, along with the rest of the Channel Islands, was for centuries in the front line of wars between England and France. First ruled by the Dukes of Normandy, Guernsey retained its ancient laws and privileges as a reward for its loyalty to the English crown in the 13th century. Since then, the Bailiwick of Guernsey, which also includes Alderney, Herm and Sark, has been a self-governing dependency of the British crown. Today, with its equable climate, natural beauty and low taxation, this little island prospers as a tourist destination, a haven for wealthy residents and a base for banking and insurance industries.

HISTORY

Neolithic burial chambers and artefacts such as arrow heads found on Guernsey show that the island has been occupied by man for the last 7,000 years. Several well preserved examples of these burial chambers, or dolmens, can be seen today including the largest, La Varde Dolmen, on L'Ancresse Common in the north of the island. Earthworks and artefacts dating from the later Iron Age have also been found in the southeast of the island. Other archaeological remains, including large amounts of pottery that have been found around St Peter Port harbour, show that Guernsey was an important staging post for traders sailing between France and England in Roman times.

Christianity came to Guernsey in the 6th century, when St Sampson founded a church on the island. During the 9th century, the region had come under attack from the Vikings and by 911AD their leader, Rollo, controlled most of Normandy. By 933AD his son, William Longsword, had annexed the Channel Islands into what became the Duchy of Normandy. When William Longsword's successor, William the Conqueror, invaded England in 1066, the Channel Islands came under the control of the English crown and were ruled from London. In 1204, when King John lost

Left and below *The picturesque town of St Peter Port, with its elegant 19th century houses and narrow cobbled streets, is set on a hill overlooking the busy harbour. Regular ferry services operate from here to Sark, Herm, Jersey and the UK mainland.*

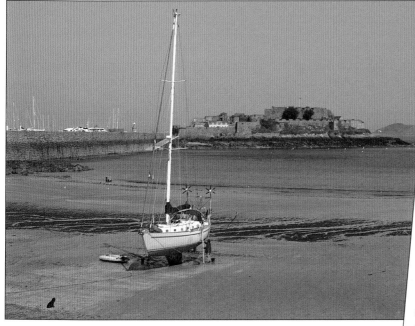

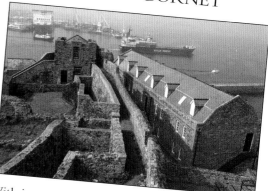

CASTLE CORNET

With its commanding view over St Peter Port Harbour, Castle Cornet dates back to the late 13th century when it was built by King John to protect Guernsey against French invasion. Home to the island's Governor and the scene of a nine year siege during the English Civil War, the castle was seriously damaged when lightning struck an underground gunpowder magazine in 1672. Later rebuilt and extended during the 18th century, Castle Cornet was connected to the mainland by a causeway in 1860. The castle and its six museums are open to the public.

Above *With Castle Cornet as a backdrop, one man and his dog carry out maintenance to their boat on the beach at Havelet Bay in St Peter Port.*

his French territories, the Channel Islanders remained loyal to England. In return, King John rewarded them by allowing the islands to retain their ancients laws and privileges and to be almost self-governing. This situation remains to the present day with the Bailiwick of Guernsey, which also includes Alderney, Herm and Sark, being a British crown dependency.

Despite the building of Castle Cornet to protect the harbour at St Peter Port, the island of Guernsey came under attack and was seized by French forces on several occasions. Peace only settled on the island in 1483 when the Channel Islands were declared neutral by Pope Sixtus IV. It was at this time that Guernsey and Jersey were separated into the two bailiwicks that we know today.

During the English Civil War, while the rest of Guernsey sided with the Parliamentarians, the Governor, Sir Peter Osborne, and his Royalist troops remained under siege in Castle Cornet for nine years until they surrendered in 1651.

Under its self-governing and neutral status, by the 16th century Guernsey had become a centre for legalised smuggling between France and England. This lucrative trade ended in 1689, when the island's neutral status was suspended. However, both the fishing and associated knitwear industries continued to prosper and, by the 18th century, Guernsey shipowners had also ventured into the lucrative, but dangerous, business of privateering.

By the early 19th century, the war between England and France brought many unwelcome changes to the people of Guernsey. Unemployment, together

with an influx of refugees from Napoleon's France, led to great hardships which were to continue until 1815. Dating from this period, the string of defensive forts and Martello towers that can be seen today along Guernsey's coastline were further strengthened during the mid-19th century when another war with France was threatened.

With the end of the war, prosperity returned to Guernsey. New roads were built, St Peter Port harbour was enlarged and new industries such as the growing and export of glasshouse tomatoes and stone quarrying were born. With the introduction of regular ferry services by the Great Western Railway from

Above *Fort Grey, also known as the Chateau de Rocquaine, was built in 1804 during the war with France. With a commanding view over Rocquaine Bay, its Martello Tower now houses a Shipwreck Museum.*

Below *Also built during the Napoleonic War, Martello Tower No 4 overlooks the broad sandy sweep of L'Ancresse and Pembroke Bays in the far north of Guernsey.*

Weymouth in 1857, Guernsey prospered as an important destination not only for tourists, but also for wealthy new residents. This link was also vital to the growth of the important glasshouse industry on the island, which could now deliver its fresh produce directly to the London markets.

The outbreak of World War II brought an end to Guernsey's prosperity. By 1940, with German forces already in northern France, it was only a matter of time before the undefended Channel Islands were invaded. St Peter Port was bombed on 28 June 1940 and, two days later, a platoon of German soldiers landed unopposed at Guernsey Airport. Thus began almost five years of German occupation. Guernsey, along with the rest of the Channel Islands, was turned once again into an an armed fortress with concrete coastal batteries, observation posts and underground facilities being built by armies of European slave workers. The Channel Islands were bypassed during the Allied invasion of France in June 1944 and, cut off from their supply route, both the 13,000 German troops and 23,000 civilians on Guernsey faced starvation. Finally, the Red Cross chartered a Swedish ship, *Vega*, which was allowed to bring Red Cross food parcels into St Peter Port in December 1944. The occupation of Guernsey ended when German forces surrendered on 9 May 1945.

Since the end of the war, Guernsey's prosperity has returned and today, while tourism is still important, financial services such as offshore banking and insurance account for over half of the island's income.

NATURAL HISTORY

Although heavily populated, the island of Guernsey possesses a wide range of natural habitats. With the setting up of many nature reserves, much has been achieved in recent years to protect many of these habitats. During spring and early summer, the rugged south coast with its steep cliffs, sheltered bays and wooded valleys supports a wide variety of wild flowers and birdlife. The numerous headlands along this coast are favourite spots for birdwatchers during the spring and autumn migration season and, at Pleinmont Point, they may be lucky enough to see a rare Dartford warbler nesting in the gorse bushes.

With its long sandy beaches and rocky headlands, Guernsey's west coast is home

Right *Set on a headland overlooking Vazon and Cobo Bays on Guernsey's north coast, Fort Hommet contains an interesting mixture of 19th century Victorian fortifications and concrete gun emplacements built by the Germans in 1942.*

to many wading birds during the winter months. The headland at Fort Hommet has been designated as a nature reserve and, during the spring and early summer, this area of sand dune, heathland and saltmarsh supports many rare plants.

Inland from the southwest coast there are three other nature reserves: Silbe Nature Reserve is an area of woodland; and La Claire Mare and the Colin Best Nature Reserves are both important areas of marshland and reedbed.

Again on the west coast and reached by a tidal causeway from Fort Saumarez, the small island of Lihou is another important protected site for resident and migrant birds, as well as many rare species of maritime plants.

In the north of the island, the Vale Pond and Le Grand Pré Nature Reserves, with their saltmarshes and reedbeds, also attract large numbers of migrant birds and overwintering waders. An area of grassland and sand dunes, the reserve at Port Soif is famed for its many rare species of wild orchid that flower here in early summer.

HOW TO GET THERE
By air There are direct flights to Guernsey from many airports in the UK and from Jersey, Alderney, Dinard, St Brieuc, Rotterdam, Dusseldorf and Stuttgart.
By sea Condor Ferries operate a regular high-speed catamaran service to Guernsey from Weymouth, Poole, Portsmouth, Jersey and St Malo. For more details contact their reservations office (tel. 0870 243 5140) or visit their website: www.condorferries.com

Manche Iles Express operate a high speed catamaran service to Guernsey from Dielette in the Cherbourg

peninsula. For more details contact their Guernsey office (tel. 01481 701316), or visit their website: www.manche-iles-express.com

TOURIST INFORMATION
Guernsey Tourist Board, North Esplanade, St Peter Port, Guernsey GY1 3AN (tel. 01481 723552) or visit their website: www.visitguernsey.com

WHERE TO STAY
Guernsey offers a wide variety of accommodation, from hotels and guesthouses to self-catering units and campsites. For further details contact the Guernsey Tourist Board (see above).

ISLAND WALKS
Guernsey is covered in a network of roads and lanes, some of which can be quite busy at times. However, a 10-mile footpath traverses the whole length of the island's dramatic south coast between Jerbourg Point in the southeast to Portelet Harbour in the southwest. A series of footpaths also link Le Grand Havre around the north coast to Fort

Doyle. An excellent circular bus service around the island enables walkers to choose start and finish points to suit their own itinerary.

PLACES TO VISIT
● La Vallette Underground Military Museum
● Sausmarez Manor
● Castle Cornet
● Maison Victor Hugo
● German Naval Signals Headquarters
● Guernsey Telephone Museum
● Little Chapel
● German Occupation Museum
● Fort Grey
● Lihou Island
● La Varde Dolmen

SHELL CHAPEL

Based on the Grotto at Lourdes, the Little Chapel was started in 1914 by Brother Deodat of the religious order 'The Brothers of the Christian Schools'. The present building, covered in thousands of tiny pebbles and china fragments, is the third chapel built on the site at Les Vauxbelets. The chapel is now under the care of the nearby Blanchelande Girls' College and is open to the public.

HERM

Once a Neolithic burial ground, tiny Herm was first ruled by the Dukes of Normandy in the 10th century and inhabited by monks and farmers. It later became a sporting playground for the Governors of Guernsey until becoming a centre for granite quarrying in the 19th century. Following periods of private ownership and German wartime occupation, Herm's natural beauty and tourist facilities now attract thousands of visitors each year.

Above *Traversing the spine of Herm from north to south, this quiet farm track passes through pinewoods and the agricultural heart of the island. After tourism, dairy farming is the most important employer on Herm.*

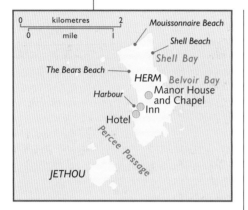

HISTORY

Evidence in the form of a large number of neolithic tombs, and artefacts such as tools and weapons found in the north of Herm, show that the island has been occupied by man for at least 5,000 years. Other evidence has been unearthed to show that Roman traders also visited the island about 2,000 years ago. During the 6th century, Herm was used as a place of meditation for early monks from Jersey and Sark, who built a small chapel here. By the 10th century, Herm was ruled by the Dukes of Normandy and eventually came under the control of the Benedictine abbey of Mont St Michel. It was during the 12th century that the present church on Herm, dedicated to the early Celtic missionary St Tugual, was built on the site of the earlier chapel. From 1204 Herm, along with the rest of the Channel Islands, came under the control of the English Crown.

From the 16th century until 1737, Herm was used as a sporting playground for the Governors of Guernsey. Stocked with game birds and rabbits, the island became a favourite haunt for the wealthy hunting, shooting and fishing fraternity from Guernsey. In the 19th century, granite quarries were established on the island and a large comnmunity

infrastructure was established to support the 400 or so quarrymen and their families. Until the 1880s, Herm granite was much in demand, and exported to England for use in the building of roads and bridges. The quarries fell into disuse and, from 1889 until 1949, Herm was owned by a succession of famous people including Prince Blücher von Wahlstatt, grandson of the famous Marshall Blücher who fought with the British at the Battle of Waterloo, the novelist Compton Mackenzie and Sir Percival Perry, chairman of the Ford Motor Company.

During World War II Herm, along with the rest of the Channel Islands, was occupied by German forces. It was liberated in 1945, and from 1949 was

Above *Visitors to Herm pass through this imposing granite gateway on their climb to St Tugual's Church on the summit of the island.*

Right *The island's paths and tracks are well signposted. Attractive beach cafes are located at the southern end of Shell Bay and, here, at smaller Belvoir Bay.*

Right *Sculpted by the wind and sea, these granite outcrops overlook the deserted Mouisonniere Beach at the north of the island.*

leased by the States of Guernsey to Peter and Jenny Wood. They and their family, who now manage Herm, have successfully preserved the island's beauty while improving facilities for its many thousands of visitors.

NATURAL HISTORY

Although only a small island, Herm possesses an abundance of natural habitats, ranging from sand dunes, maritime heath, grassland and woodland to sandy beaches, rock pools and steep granite cliffs.

Both Herm's hinterland and coastline are a paradise for bird lovers. In addition to its resident birds such as robin, wren, blackbird, thrush, kestrel and the rarer long-eared owl, the island is visited by many migrants from southern Europe and North Africa in the spring. Covered in yellow gorse during summer, the upland areas of the island provide an ideal home for visitors such as whitethroat, willow warbler and whinchat. The northern half of the island's coastline sees turnstone, oystercatcher, curlew, and, during the winter, Brent goose. The cliffs and rocky islets around the southern half of the island are home to colonies of guillemot, razorbill, shag, cormorant and the occasional puffin.

Herm's many natural habitats also support over 450 different plant species. During summer the island is ablaze with the colour of bright yellow gorse and clifftop flowers such as sea and red campion, heather and foxglove. The flat northern part of the island, known as The Common, is covered in rockrose and many other tiny flowers, while the sand dunes that fringe the shoreline have been planted with marram grass in an attempt to halt erosion.

HOW TO GET THERE

From April to October there is a regular boat service for the 20 minute crossing from St Peter Port, Guernsey. A limited service also operates from November to March. For more details visit the island's website: www.herm-island.com

For information on how to get to Guernsey, see page 17.

TOURIST INFORMATION

For details on tourist information visit the island's website: www.herm-island.com

WHERE TO STAY

In addition to the White House Hotel, there are 20 self-catering cottages and apartments and one campsite on Herm. For details of all of these visit the island's website: www.herm-island.com

ISLAND WALKS

Apart from a few farm tractors, Herm is traffic-free. From either of the two landing points (Rosaire Landing at low tide and The Harbour at high tide), a footpath traverses the entire coastline of the island, a distance of about four miles. Several other tracks and footpaths cross the centre of the island from north to south and from west to east.

PLACES TO VISIT
● Mermaid Tavern
● Shell Beach
● St Tugual's Church
● Pierre aux Rats obelisk

Above *Along the northeast coast, the expanse of Shell Beach is one of Herm's most popular attractions. The beach is made up of sand and fragments of hundreds of different types of shell washed up by the Gulf Stream.*

JETHOU

Separated from the southwest coast of Herm by a narrow channel, the tiny island of Jethou has recently become a secluded retreat for its wealthy tenants. On the eastern slopes, Fairy Wood and its standing stone are thought to have been used by Druids for their pagan ceremonies. Jethou's many previous tenants include the novelist Compton Mackenzie who moved there in 1923 after selling the lease of Herm to Sir Percival Perry, then chairman of the Ford Motor Company. From 1964 until 1971, the island was owned by the Faed family and boasted a cafe and restaurant open to the public.

SARK

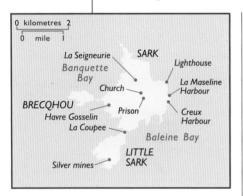

The last feudal state in Europe and once a pirate stronghold, Sark was fought over for centuries by the French and English until Helier de Carteret became the first seigneur, or lord of the manor, in 1563. Since then, a succession of seigneurs have ruled over their kingdom with little interference from outside until recently. Sark's uniqueness and natural beauty have guaranteed that tourism is the most important economic activity on the island today.

Above *The two harbours on the east coast of Sark, Masseline and Creux, are linked via tunnels to the steep road that leads up to the main settlement. The tunnel to Creux Harbour, above, was cut in 1866, while a second tunnel, now disused, dates from 1588.*

HISTORY

Archæological evidence, in the form of two megalithic tombs, weapons and tools discovered on Sark, shows that the island has probably been occupied for about 4,000 years. The Sark Hoard – an earthenware pot containing metal objects and coins – was discovered on the island in 1719 and dates from the early Roman period. It is thought that Sark, along with rest of the Channel Islands, was administered by the Romans from the Norman town of Coutances. During the 6th century,

the early Christian missionary St Magloire founded a monastery on the island, and this continued to operate until it was destroyed by Viking raiders in the 9th century. By the 10th century, Sark was ruled by the Dukes of Normandy and subsequently, following the Norman invasion of England in 1066, came under the control of the English Crown.

From the 14th century until the mid-16th century, Sark was not only a haven for pirates, but was also invaded and occupied by French forces on many occasions. In 1563, Helier de Carteret, a feudal ruler from St Ouen on Jersey, was granted permission by the English Crown to settle on Sark. Building himself a manor house, de Carteret created 35 farming tenements and, within a few years, was reaping the rewards from his tiny feudal kingdom. Although officially under the control of the Bailiwick of Guernsey, Sark set up its own government, or Chief Pleas, in 1579. Sark's short period of independence did not last long and, in 1582, was put down by armed men and officers from

Guernsey. A year later, a compromise was reached which allowed the people of Sark to set up their own elected court, albeit still coming under the jurisdiction of Guernsey. Only interrupted by the English Civil War, the de Carteret family provided a long line of seigneurs until the death of Lord John Carteret in 1720.

After the long line of de Carteret seigneurships, a succession of good, bad, indifferent and sometimes eccentric lords of the manor ruled the island for over 200 years. In 1927, following her father's death, Sark's most famous lord of the manor, Dame Sibyl Hathaway, took her seat in the Chief Pleas. Apart from the period of the German Occupation of Sark between 1940 and 1945, Dame Sibyl oversaw major changes on the island, the most important being

BRECQHOU

Separated from the west coast of Sark by the narrow Gouliot Passage, the island of Brecqhou is one of the 40 freehold properties in Sark that give the owner a seat on the island's government or Chief Pleas. Free from any income tax, this 160–acre island is currently owned by the multi-millionaire Barclay brothers who have turned Brecqhou into a private impregnable fortress complete with a gothic-style castle. Visitors are not welcome!

Right *Opposite the island of Brecqhou, the sheltered jetty at Havre Gosselin is an alternative landing point for boats from Guernsey when the main harbours on the east coast of Sark are closed by bad weather.*

improvements to the infrastructure and the development of the offshore banking and tourist industries. Sark's ancient feudal system, long under attack from the European Union for its denial of human rights and representation, was replaced by a more democratic body in 2006.

NATURAL HISTORY

Best viewed from the sea, Sark's rugged cliffs and numerous rocky islets support large colonies of seabirds during the breeding season. As well as guillemot, razorbill and puffin, the keen-eyed birdwatcher might also see a colony of tern, fulmar, oystercatcher and the impressive peregrine falcon.

Sark's flat plateau is a favourite stopping off point for many migrant birds during the spring and summer, and is also home to residents such as robin, wren, firecrest and birds of prey including kestrel and long-eared owl.

Over 600 species of plant and wildflower have been recorded on Sark. Untouched by modern farming methods, the island's hedgerows are filled with an abundance of wildflowers during spring and summer. In early summer the cliffs are covered in bluebell, red campion and foxglove.

There are no reptiles on Sark, but the mammal population includes rabbit, hedgehog, the lesser white-toothed shrew, field mouse, pipistrelle bat and the rare black rat.

Below *With 260ft drops on either side, this mist-shrouded causeway, known as La Coupée, links Sark with Little Sark. It was built across a narrow isthmus by German prisoners of war after World War II.*

Above *Open to the public, the walled gardens at the manor house, La Seigneurie, were created by the Dame of Sark, Sibyl Hathaway (1884-1974). The house was built by Helier de Carteret in 1565 and further extended in the 18th century. It is the official residence of the current Seigneur of Sark, Michael Beaumont.*

HOW TO GET THERE

There is a regular, all year round, boat service for the 45 minute crossing from St Peter Port, Guernsey. For more details contact the Isle of Sark Shipping Company (tel. 01481 724059) or visit their website: www.sarkshipping.guernsey.net During the summer, there are also direct sailings from Jersey to Sark. For more information contact Manche Iles Express (tel. 01534 888783) or visit their website: www.manche-iles-express.com

For information on how to get to Guernsey, see page 17.

TOURIST INFORMATION

For details on tourist information contact the island's information office (tel. 01481 832345) or visit their website: www.sark.info

WHERE TO STAY

There is a wide range of accommodation available on Sark, ranging from hotels and guesthouses to a campsite. For details contact the island's information office (see above).

ISLAND WALKS

Apart from farm tractors and horse-drawn carriages, Sark is traffic-free. For the walker, there is a good network of well-signposted unmetalled roads, tracks and footpaths on the island. A good way to see the island is by bicycle, and there are several hire shops to be found at the top of the hill leading from the harbour.

PLACES TO VISIT
● La Seigneurie Gardens
● La Coupée
● Occupation and heritage museum
● 19th century St Peter's Church

SARK PRISON

Built in 1856, Sark's tiny prison is the smallest in the world and can only accommodate two people. The island's policeman, or Connetable, has the power to hold somebody in this jail for up to 48 hours, after which they must be released or moved to Guernsey for trial.

ALDERNEY

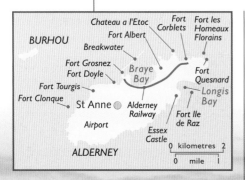

Located only nine miles from the French coast, it is hardly surprising that little Alderney has been in the front line during centuries of bitter European conflict. Turned into an armed fortress during the 19th century, Alderney became a vast concentration camp during the German occupation in World War II. Today, tourism is the main economic activity, with the island's natural beauty, historical legacy and rich diversity of flora and birdlife attracting thousands of visitors each year.

HISTORY

Lying only nine miles from the coast of France, the island of Alderney was used during the Neolithic and Iron Age periods as a burial ground for prehistoric man. Although evidence in the form of artefacts has been unearthed, most of the tombs were destroyed in more recent times by the building of the forts and other military structures that are found all over the island. Alderney later became an important staging post for the

Romans, who built a fort overlooking their harbour at Longis Bay.

Little is known of the history of Alderney until the 10th century, when it came under the control of the Dukes of Normandy. In the 11th century, the island was granted to the Abbot of Mont St Michel, but a later charter transferred half to the Bishop of Coutances with the other half being retained by the Dukes. Although Alderney eventually fell under the auspices of the English Crown, religious control was still exercised from France until the 16th century. Unique to the Channel Islands, Alderney was not under feudal rule but, from the 16th to the 19th centuries, was controlled by a Crown-appointed Governor.

Due to its proximity to France, Alderney was constantly in the front line in the wars between the French and English, and on several occasions during the 14th and 16th centuries, the island

Above *Set on a hill overlooking Braye Harbour, the capital of Alderney, St Anne, was oiginally a medieval farming settlement. Its narrow cobbled streets and painted 19th century houses exude a distinctly French flavour.*

was temporarily seized by French forces. The first fortifications to protect the island were started by Henry VIII, but the most enduring are those that were built during the threat of invasion from France in the 19th century.

Between 1847 and 1870, Alderney was turned into an enormous building site. Using locally quarried stone, thousands of workmen constructed 12 forts stretching along the north coast, from Clonque Bay round to Longis Bay on

Below *On a headland overlooking Saye Bay, Fort Chateau a L'Etoc is one of the many fortifications built on Alderney during the 19th century.*

Right *This massive concrete fortification overlooking Mannez Quarry stands as stark testimony to the German occupation of Alderney during World War II.*

the south. A railway was also built to carry stone from Mannez Quarry to the enormous breakwater that was being built at Braye. The harbour that was formed by this was large enough to accommodate the whole of the British Channel fleet. The expected invasion never came, but a large garrison remained stationed on the island until 1930.

Quarrying remained an important industry on Alderney until World War II, and huge quantities of granite for use in road construction were exported from Braye Harbour. With around 40 farms on the island, farming also played an important role in the island's economy. Self-supporting in dairy products, poultry and pigs, these farms also reared and exported cattle. Tourism, vital to the island's ecomomy today, had also started to develop during the latter part of the 19th century and, with improved air and sea links, had become a flourishing industry by the outbreak of World War II.

Alderney's darkest hour came during World War II. On 23 June 1940, with the threat of imminent German invasion hanging over them, the vast majority of Alderney's population were evacuated to Weymouth, and the island's cattle taken to Guernsey. German forces landed unopposed on the virtually deserted island only nine days later. In 1941, Hitler decreed that the Channel Islands

should be fortified against possible British attack. Within a short time, the Germans had set up four large camps on Alderney and filled them with thousands of slave workers from their conquered lands in Europe. Appallingly treated by their German captors, over 7,000 of these workers, mainly Russians, Poles and Jews, perished on the island. The massive and virtually indestructible concrete structures built on Alderney by these poor people are a constant reminder today of the horrors of war. Bypassed by the Allied landings in northern France in June 1944, Alderney and the rest of the Channel Islands soon became cut off from the war in Europe. The Germans on Alderney surrendered to the liberating British forces on 16 May 1945, and a massive operation began to make the island a safe place for its exiled inhabitants. Assisted by German prisoners of war, British troops cleared miles of barbed wire and destroyed over 35,000

mines. Buildings were repaired, 300 homes were made habitable and, by the summer of 1946, most of the islanders had returned.

During the rehabilitation of Alderney, the island was run as a communal farm until 1949, when the Government of Alderney Law 1948 came into force. With a written constitution, this Act imposed taxes on the island's people for the first time. Responsibilty for administration and providing services was divided between the island and the Bailiwick of Guernsey.

Today, the island's equable climate, natural beauty and historical legacy attract thousands of visitors every year. Additionally, its low taxation rates have also encouraged many retired people from mainland Britain to settle here. While tourism is still the most important economic activity on the island, recent years have also seen a growth in the finance industry and e-commerce.

NATURAL HISTORY

Only three miles long and, at its widest point, just over one mile wide, Alderney supports a wide range of habitats, from heathland and freshwater lakes to rocky seashore, cliffs and many offshore islets. A paradise for the birdwatcher, over 250 species of bird have been recorded on the island, including many rare sightings during the spring and autumn migration seasons. During the breeding season, colonies of seabirds including shag, puffin, razorbill, guillemot, gannet and fulmar make their home on the cliffs, rock stacks and offshore islets. One of these, Burhou, has its own warden to watch over the colonies of Atlantic grey seal, storm petrel and puffin that breed here in late spring and summer. Alderney's seashore is also an important site for overwintering waders such as turnstone and dunlin, along with the resident oystercatcher.

Alderney's large resident bird population includes birds of prey such as kestrel and a few pairs of peregrine. The clifftops and heathland also support skylark, stonechat and linnet while the extremely rare fan-tailed and Dartford warbler also nest on the island.

The island is also a delight for the botanist, with over 900 species, some rare and endangered, being recorded here. During spring and summer, the island is covered with a colourful array of wildflowers from bright yellow gorse and spotted rock rose to pink thrift and pyramidal orchid. Unique to Alderney are the Alderney geranium and Alderney sea-lavender.

Unlike the rich diversity of flora to be found on the island, Alderney's mammal population is more limited. Of significance to the island is the flea-free blonde hedgehog, the greater white tooth shrew and a large population of pipistrelle bat. There are no reptiles on Alderney apart from the slow worm.

The Alderney Wildlife Trust actively promotes the conservation and protection of the island's habitats and terrestrial and marine wildlife. For more information about the Trust visit their website: www.alderneywildlife.org

HOW TO GET THERE

By air Aurigny (tel. 01481 822886) operate regular services to Alderney from Guernsey and Southampton. For details visit their website: www.aurigny.com

Blue Islands (tel. 01481 727567) operate regular services from Guernsey, Jersey, Bournemouth, Brighton (Shoreham) and St Brieuc. For more details visit their website: www.blueislands.com

By sea Between April and the end of September, Manche Iles Express operate a high speed catamaran service to Alderney from Dielette in the Cherbourg peninsula and Guernsey. For more details contact their Guernsey office (01481 701316), or visit their website: www.manche-iles-express.com

TOURIST INFORMATION

Alderney Tourism Office, Queen Elizabeth II Street, Alderney GY9 3AA (tel. 01481 822811/823737) or visit their website: www.alderney.net

WHERE TO STAY

Alderney offers a wide variety of accommodation, from a camp site to self-catering cottages and apartments, guesthouses and hotels. For further details contact the Alderney Tourism Office (see above).

ISLAND WALKS

Unlike Guernsey and Jersey, the roads on Alderney are fairly quiet. These, together with a good network of tracks and paths, make it possible to enjoy the island and its beautiful coastline on foot. Bicycle hire is also available.

PLACES TO VISIT

● Alderney Museum, St Anne
● Alderney Railway
● Victorian forts including Fort Ile de Raz, Fort les Homeaux Florain, Fort Corblets, Fort Albert and Fort Doyle
● German World War II defences overlooking Mannez Quarry
● Braye harbour and breakwater

Below *The rusting railway lines perching precariously on Braye breakwater once carried trains loaded with granite from Mannez Quarry. During the winter of 1911/1912, a loaded train ran off the end of the breakwater and after that incident, all locomotives travelling along it had to carry lifebelts.*

Above *Originally nearly a mile long, the 2,854ft-long breakwater that encloses Braye Harbour was built during a period of heightened tension between France and England in the 19th century. Large enough to accommodate the British Channel fleet at that time, it took nearly 20 years to complete. A planned eastern breakwater to totally enclose the harbour never materialised.*

THE ALDERNEY RAILWAY

Opened in 1847 to carry stone from Mannez Quarry for the construction of forts and the Braye breakwater, the standard gauge Alderney Railway was operated for many years by the British Admiralty. In 1980, the two-mile line was leased from the Home Office by the Alderney Railway Society. The railway is now open to the public between Easter and end of September, with trains departing from Braye Road station (above) for the journey to Mannez Quarry. Passengers are conveyed in former London Underground cars pushed and pulled by a small diesel locomotive.

Below *Peace and solitude on the deserted white, sandy beaches of the Isles of Scilly, such as Green Bay on Bryher, are some of the many attractions that draw visitors to the islands of South West England. From the breathtaking beauty of the Scillies and the Art Deco experience of tiny Burgh Island, to the rugged remoteness of Lundy and the fascinating history of Steep Holm - each island has its own uniqueness and character.*

SOUTH WEST ENGLAND

STEEP HOLM
LUNDY ISLAND
ISLES OF SCILLY
ST MICHAEL'S MOUNT
LOOE ISLAND
BURGH ISLAND

STEEP HOLM

Once a place of meditation and prayer, the tiny island of Steep Holm appears like a giant beached whale in the Bristol Channel. Its limestone cliffs provide sanctuary to thousands of nesting seabirds and its 250ft high plateau is home to many rare herbal and medicinal plants. Used as a base by marauding Vikings and, during the Middle Ages, as a commercial rabbit warren by English noblemen, for centuries the island was the haunt of fishermen and smugglers. Still littered with 19th and 20th century military relics, Steep Holm has twice been turned into an armed fortress during times of potential and actual war. Apart from wartime, the island has been a nature reserve since the 1930s. Steep Holm's rich historical legacy and unique flora and fauna were finally saved for posterity when the island was sold to the Kenneth Allsop Memorial Trust in 1976.

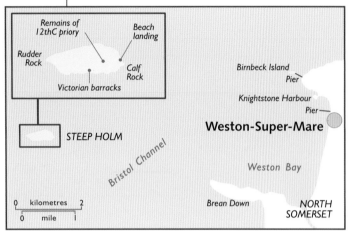

HISTORY

It is thought that Iron Age hunters and fishermen probably visited Steep Holm at least 2,500 years ago. Archæologists have also discovered Roman artefacts including pottery and coins on the island, as well as the remains of a signal station at the western end, high above Rudder Rock.

During the 6th century, early Christian monks from South Wales, led by St Gildas, spent time on Steep Holm in prayer and meditation. However, the peace and solitude of the region was

shattered in the latter part of the 9th century by the arrival of Viking raiders. Probably using Steep Holm as a base, they sailed up the River Severn to plunder and terrorise the Anglo-Saxon settlements along its banks. Peace had returned to the region by the time of the Norman invasion in the 11th century.

During the 12th century the Lord of Uphill Manor, on the nearby mainland, had a small Augustinian priory erected on Steep Holm. Life for the small number of monks on the island was tough

and the priory had closed by 1260. Visitors to the island can see excavation work in progress on the priory site. By 1315, Steep Holm was owned by the Lords of Berkeley who lived in Berkeley Castle in Gloucestershire. The Berkeleys set up a rabbit warren on the island to supply fur and meat which continued in use for over 300 years – even though the island

Right *During World War II, several searchlight posts, like this one at Rudder Rock, were built on Steep Holm. Set low down the cliffs so that their beams could silhouette shipping, they were accessed from above by a dangerously steep flight of concrete steps.*

changed hands several time during this period due to family feuds or treasonable acts by its owners. Between 1700 and 1830 Steep Holm was owned by the Freke family from Bristol and let to tenants who made their living from fishing and collecting seabird eggs.

In 1830, Steep Holm changed hands again. This time it was bought by a local developer from Weston-super-Mare who set about building a harbour, inn and cottage and improved access to the plateau. Soon after the work was

Below *The English island of Steep Holm as seen from a Victorian gun battery on its Welsh neighbour, Flat Holm. Lying just over two miles apart in the Bristol Channel, each island has its own unique character. However, their strategic importance during the time of wars led them both to be developed into armed fortresses.*

completed the island was sold for a tidy profit to a wealthy Somerset landowner and stayed in the ownership of his descendants until 1976. Over these years Steep Holm was let to a succession of tenants and their families, who made their living with varying degrees of success from boating, fishing, farming, innkeeping and, during the 18th century, a spot of smuggling. During the 1930s, the island was turned into a nature reserve by its last tenant.

The islanders' peaceful existence, however, was twice shattered during times of potential and actual war. In the 1860s when Britain feared attack from France, a series of armed fortifications were built at the entrance to the Bristol Channel. One of these was on Steep Holm where 7-inch muzzle-loading cannons were installed in a series of batteries around the edge of the plateau.

In addition to the gun emplacements and underground ammunition stores, the military built a substantial stone garrison for the men stationed on the island. The predicted war with France never materialised and the depleted garrison was closed in 1900.

During World War II, Steep Holm was in the front line of the defence of Britain. Starting in 1941, army engineers installed four 6-inch naval guns, dating from World War I, together with their emplacements, lookouts and ammunition stores, at strategic points around the edge of the island plateau. A new landing pier was linked to the plateau by the construction of a narrow gauge switchback railway. Until 1943, up to 300 soldiers were stationed on the island, including a company of Indian sepoys and their mules, and quartered in newly-built Nissen huts.

KENNETH ALLSOP

Kenneth Allsop, 1971

STEEP HOLM 18ᴾ

Following the sudden death of broadcaster, author and conservationist Kenneth Allsop in 1973, donations to his memorial fund were used to purchase Steep Holm. A Site of Special Scientific Interest and a mecca for ornithologists, the island was sold to the Kenneth Allsop Memorial Trust for £10,000 in 1976. With a resident warden, the trust has overseen many projects designed to preserve the island's unique character.

During the 1930s, the island had been turned into a nature reserve by its last tenant and soon after the end of World War II it was leased to the Steep Holm Trust, a collection of bodies interested in preserving the island's rich historical legacy and its flora and fauna. Finally, in 1976, the island was purchased by the Kenneth Allsop Memorial Trust in memory of the broadcaster, author and conservationist who had died three years earlier. Since then, the Trust has been involved in extensive clearance, restoration and conservation work.

NATURAL HISTORY

During the breeding season in the spring and early summer, Steep Holm's steep limestone cliffs provide safe sanctuary for colonies of seabirds, including herring gulls, lesser black-headed gulls and cormorants. Migrating birds also pause to rest on the island during the spring and autumn seasons. Although the rabbits have long since died out, a small herd of shy Muntjac deer, introduced some years ago, still inhabit the island.

Botanists, including Sir Joseph Banks, have been visiting Steep Holm since the late 18th century. They found that the island was home to *paeonia mascula*, a plant normally found in more southern, Mediterranean climates. It is thought that the peony was introduced by monks in the 12th century. The 'Steep Holm Peony', along with a profusion of other plants originally introduced for their herbal and medicinal qualities such as the wild leek and wild turnip, can still be seen growing on the island today.

HOW TO GET THERE

Boat trips to land on Steep Holm are organised by the Kenneth Allsop Memorial Trust. Trips run from the end of May to September and depart from Knightstone Harbour in Weston-super-Mare. No dogs are allowed on the island. Advance booking is essential. For details contact the Kenneth Allsop Memorial Trust (tel. 01934 632307).

ORDNANCE SURVEY MAPS

Landranger 1:50,000 series Nos. 182

TOURIST INFORMATION

Weston-super-Mare Tourist Information Centre, Beach Lawns Beach Rd Weston-Super-Mare, BS23 1AT (tel. 01934 888800). Website: www.somersetcoast.com

WHERE TO STAY

There is no accommodation on Steep Holm. For details of accommodation in Weston-super-Mare contact the Tourist Information Centre (see above).

ISLAND WALKS

From the landing beach, a steep path leads up to the plateau where there are extensive views across the Bristol Channel. A path takes visitors around the perimeter of the plateau, with several steep diversions to places of interest.

PLACES TO VISIT

- Victorian Barracks
- Remains of Victorian and World War II gun emplacements
- Remains of Roman signal station
- Site of 12th century priory

Above *Fearing war with France, Steep Holm, its neighbour Flat Holm and the headlands on either side of the Bristol Channel all became armed fortresses during the 1860s. Scattered around Steep Holm are the remains of gun batteries, underground ammunition stores and 7-ton cannons. The pivot for this gun at Split Rock Battery was a Georgian cannon sunk into the ground.*

Left *Archaelogists excavate the site of a 12th century Augustinian priory on Steep Holm. Although the monks did not stay long, the building was occupied again in the 14th century by Lord Berkeley's men who raised rabbits on the island.*

Below *During World War II, several batteries of 6-inch naval guns were installed on Steep Holm. At Summit Battery this massive concrete structure complete with rusted securing bolts has a commanding view over the approaches to Cardiff and neighbouring Flat Holm.*

Lundy Island

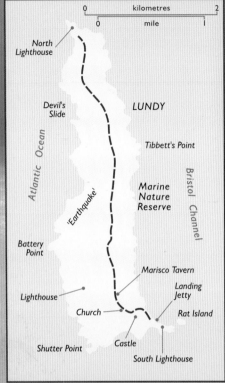

Three miles long and half a mile wide, Lundy Island lies 10 miles off the coast of North Devon. For hundreds of years its high granite cliffs provided sanctuary for bands of pirates and smugglers. However, after many changes of ownership, peace finally descended on the island in the 19th century. Owned by the National Trust since 1976, Lundy Island is leased to the Landmark Trust. Today, the island attracts visitors not only for its solitude and beauty but also for its rich historical legacy and unique natural habitats.

History

Lundy has been inhabited since prehistoric times and traces of Bronze and Iron Age settlements have been discovered on the island. After the end of Roman rule in Britain, an early Christian community survived on the island and standing stones from this period can still be seen in the cemetery. During the 9th century, Viking boats were making forays into the Bristol Channel and the island of Lundy, known by the Vikings as Puffin Island, is mentioned in a famous Norse saga from that time. By the mid-12th century, a Norman family, the Mariscos, had settled on the island. They later refused to hand Lundy over to Henry II and it became a pirate stronghold for the next 100 years. To put an end to the Mariscos' troublemaking, Henry III finally captured the island and built a castle at the southern end.

Over the next four centuries, Lundy changed hands several times and became a haven for pirates and smugglers. Peace finally settled on Lundy in 1834, when the island was purchased by William Hudson Heaven. In an attempt to bring employment to Lundy, Heaven opened granite quarries on the east side of the island in 1863. These did not prove to be commercially viable and were closed in 1868. William Heaven died in 1883 and was succeeded by his son, Reverend Hudson Heaven. In 1896, using granite from the disused quarries, Trinity House completed the North and South lighthouses. Lundy changed hands again

Right *Introduced in 1929 by Martin Harman, Lundy stamps are still officially used today and are sold in 'Puffin' values of 1 puffin = 1 pence*

Above *The path along the east coast of Lundy offers magnificent views over the Marine Nature Reserve. An ill-fated scheme to quarry granite from these cliffs in the 1860s was short-lived. The old quarries and the trackbed of a horse-drawn tramway can still be seen today.*

in 1917 when it was bought by Augustus Christie. He, in turn, sold it to Martin Harman in 1925.

A naturalist, Martin Harman set about transforming Lundy. He introduced many animals to the island, including Soay sheep and deer. In 1929, he introduced the first Lundy stamps and an issue of coins. On his death in 1954, Lundy passed jointly to his son, Albion, and his two daughters. Albion died in 1968 and the two sisters put the island up for sale. Following an appeal and a large donation from millionaire businessman Sir Jack Hayward, the National Trust was able to purchase Lundy and lease it to the Landmark Trust. Since then, the Landmark Trust have improved services on the island for residents and visitors alike. In 1986, the waters around Lundy were designated as the first Statutory Marine Reserve in the UK.

Left *Apart from farming, the main source of income on Lundy is now from visitors. Restored by the Landmark Trust, the old granite buildings are rented as self-catering accommodation. St Helena's Church was built by the aptly named Reverend Hudson Heaven in 1897.*

Above *The Old Light was erected by Trinity House on the highest point of the island in 1819. Often obscured by cloud or sea fog, it was replaced by the South and North lights in 1897. From its lantern, visitors can enjoy spectacular views of Lundy and the North Devon coast.*

LUNDY PONIES

In 1928, the then owner of Lundy, Martin Harman introduced 50 New Forest ponies to the island. Over the years careful breeding has produced a unique breed of Lundy pony. The officially recognised herd now numbers about 20 and can be seen grazing on the plateau north of Halfway Wall. Visitors are warned not to feed these frisky animals as they have been known to kick and bite!

Below *Reached by a steep series of steps and perched on windswept granite cliffs, the remote North Light was built by Trinity House in 1897. The stone for its construction came from temporarily reopened granite quarries on the east coast. The lighthouse became unmanned in 1976 and has now been replaced by a solar powered light.*

NATURAL HISTORY

Lundy has an extremely rich and interesting flora which has been studied since the founding of the Lundy Field Society in 1946. A survey by the Society in 1971 recorded 433 species of trees and 413 species of flowering plant. The island is best known, however, for the unique Lundy cabbage which was first discovered growing on the eastern slopes in 1933. On the other hand one plant, the rhododendron, is now an unwelcome guest. Introduced to Lundy in the 1920s, these colourful but invasive plants are now being cut back by National Trust working parties each spring.

A paradise for ornithologists, Lundy has a wide variety of birdlife. The cliffs along the north and northeast coast provide nesting sites for thousands of seabirds, including herring gull, razorbill, guillemot and kittiwake. Sadly the puffin, once found in great numbers on Lundy and the island's symbol, has been in decline for several years. Curlew, meadow pipit, skylark and lapwing are among the birds that nest on Lundy's central plateau. Migrating birds, some blown thousands of miles off course, stop off for rest and recuperation on Lundy during the spring and autumn.

Rich in marine life, the waters around Lundy were designated as the first Statutory Marine Reserve in the UK in 1986. Its rare colourful species of coral and numerous sunken shipwrecks attract both divers and scientists to the island. Grey seals also breed around the coastline and large numbers of them can frequently be seen basking on the rocks at the north end of the island. Dolphins and basking sharks are also often seen in the coastal waters.

During the 1920s, the then owner of Lundy, Martin Harman, introduced many unusual animals to the island. However, only the Japanese sika deer, Soay sheep and a small herd of Lundy ponies still remain. Once domesticated, shaggy wild goats can often be seen in the most precarious positions along the clifftops.

HOW TO GET THERE

By helicopter: From early November to late March, a helicopter service operates on Mondays and Fridays from Hartland Point, Devon, to Lundy.
By sea: The *MS Oldenburg* operates from either Bideford or Ilfracombe between late March and early November.
For details of both of the above contact the Lundy Shore Office, The Quay, Bideford, Devon EX39 2LY
(tel. 01271 863636)
Website: www.lundyisland.co.uk

ORDNANCE SURVEY MAPS

Landranger 1:50,000 series No. 180

TOURIST INFORMATION

For accommodation in Bideford or Ilfracombe contact Bideford Tourist Information Centre, Victoria Park, The Quay, Bideford, North Devon (tel: 01237 477676)
Website: www.torridge.gov.uk
Ilfracombe Tourist Information Centre, Landmark Theatre, The Seafront, Ilfracombe, North Devon EX34 9BX (tel. 01271 863001)
Website: www.ilfracombe-tourism.co.uk

WHERE TO STAY

Lundy offers visitors a wide range of buildings in which to stay, ranging from a 13th century castle and a Georgian villa to a lighhouse and fisherman's chalet. There are a total of 23 self-catering properties and a campsite available. For details contact the Lundy Shore Office, The Quay, Bideford, North Devon EX39 2LY (tel. 01271 863636).
Website: www.landmarktrust.org.uk

ISLAND WALKS

A track traverses the entire length of the island from the landing jetty in the southeast corner through the main settlement and up to the northwest corner. The best way to see Lundy and enjoy the views across to North Devon is by walking around the island on the coast path, a distance of about seven miles.

PLACES TO VISIT

- St Helena's Church
- Disused granite quarries and ruins of quarrymen's hospital
- Marisco Tavern
- The Battery
- Old lighthouse
- Remains of crashed WWII bombers
- The 'Earthquake'

Above *Known as the Devil's Slide, this 400ft high slab of granite on the west coast of Lundy is a favourite spot for rock climbers.*

Below *On the west coast of Lundy, a track zig-zags steeply down to the Battery. During the 19th century, rockets and cannon were fired from here during fog to warn ships of the treacherous rocks below.*

36

Below *Late spring and early summer are the best times of the year to enjoy the colourful display of flowers, both wild and cultivated, that grow on the magical Isles of Scilly. Here, the islands of Bryher and Tresco provide a backdrop to gardens that adjoin the coastal path around The Garrison on St Mary's.*

ISLES OF SCILLY

St Mary's
St Agnes
Tresco
Bryher
St Martin's

ST MARY'S

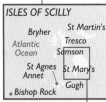

ISLES OF SCILLY

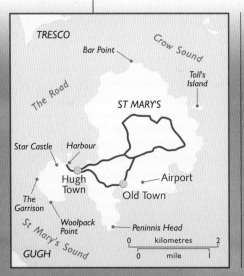

The largest and most heavily populated of the Isles of Scilly, St Mary's has always been the administrative centre of the islands. Sitting astride the converging trade routes of Britain's empire, the sheltered harbour and formidable fortifications of the capital, Hugh Town, once played an important role in protecting shipping. Where boatbuilding and flower growing were once important, St Mary's now plays an important role in support of the local tourist industry.

HISTORY

Until only a few thousand years ago, St Mary's and its near neighbours, Tresco, Bryher, Samson and St Martin's, together formed a much larger island known as Ennor. Since then, rising sea levels have formed the islands that we know today.

Although archæological remains dating from the Late Stone Age have been found on the Isles of Scilly, it was probably not until the Bronze Age (1500-500BC) that they became permanently occupied by farmers and fishermen. There are several sites on St Mary's dating from this period, including The Giant's Tomb on Porth Hellick

Down in the southeast and well-preserved chambered tombs at Halangy Down on the northwest coast and at Innisidgen on the northeast. Remains of later Iron Age occupation can also be seen on Halangy Down, where the foundations of a round house have been excavated, and at Church Point where there is a cliff castle dating from around the 5th century BC. During their occupation of Britain, the Romans certainly traded with the inhabitants of the Scillies but there is no evidence to show that they settled here.

By the 12th century, the islands had been granted to Tavistock Abbey by Henry I. They were later given to the Duchy of Cornwall but, during the reign of Elizabeth I, had been leased by Francis Godolphin. Due to its strategic importance astride the world trade routes which converged on southwest England, plans were made to build a castle to protect Hugh Town harbour. The first attempt, in the mid-16th century, was soon abandoned due to its poor position and the remains, known as Harry's Walls, can be seen today at Mount Flagon. The present Star Castle (now a hotel), with a commanding view over the harbour and its approaches, was built in the shape of an eight pointed star by Francis

Right *Between April and November, the Scillonian III operates a passenger and freight service between Penzance and St Mary's. Here, freight is being offloaded at Hugh Town for onward delivery to an outer island.*

Godolphin in 1593. Further fortifications were added over the next 300 years and, by the end of the 19th century, the little peninsula of land to the west of Hugh Town, known as The Garrison, had been turned into a heavily armed and formidable defensive stronghold.

Industrial development on St Mary's was slow. For centuries, the local population depended mainly on farming and fishing supplemented by a spot of smuggling and shipwreck salvage. By the 18th century, however, kelp burning had been developed into an important local industry. The soda and potash extracted from burnt. dried seaweed were important ingredients used in the manufacture of glass and soap on the mainland. Today, kelp pits can be seen all over the Scillies, but the best examples can be found on Toll's Island on the east coast of St Mary's.

By the early 19th century, the expansion of Britain's worldwide empire and subsequent growth in sea trade made the seas around the Scillies a focal point for shipping. A large fleet of pilot cutters,

built in St Mary's shipyards, were employed to guide ships through these dangerous waters. By 1838 there were four shipyards on the island, but by the 1880s this had all ended as more powerful, steam-driven pilots from Falmouth took over the trade. The modern decendants of the fast rowing boats, or 'gigs', which once carried pilots out to incoming ships, are still used today in inter-island races during the summer.

The growing and export of bulbs and early season cut-flowers also developed into an important source of income for the people of St Mary's during the 19th

century. Aided by the mild climate and by modern agricultural methods introduced by Augustus Smith when he leased the Scillies from the Duchy of Cornwall in 1834, this manually-intensive industry provided much-needed employment well into the 20th century.

Today, tourism is the mainstay of the local economy and provides employment for the majority of St Mary's 1,600 population. Hugh Town, the island's

Below *Hugh Town, with its shops, restaurants, pubs and busy harbour, is the main settlement on St Mary's. On the hill overlooking the harbour, the 16th century Star Castle is now a luxury hotel.*

Above and right *Perched on higher ground at Halangy Down on the northwest coast of St Mary's are the well-preserved remains of an Iron Age settlement (above) and an earlier Bronze Age chambered tomb (right). In the distance is the island of Tresco, with its fine sandy beaches and famous Abbey Gardens.*

Below *Sculpted by the wind and sea, strangely shaped granite outcrops are a feature of the coast around Peninnis Head. During the early spring and summer, this rugged section of St Mary's coastline provides landfall for many rare visiting migrant birds.*

capital and centre of administration, provides all of the necessary sevices to support this. The harbour bustles with the comings and goings of boats connecting with the outer islands and the arrival of *Scillonian III* from Penzance is always a pleasant highlight of each day. An evening stroll along The Garrison to watch the sun go down over the Atlantic followed by a few pints in one of Hugh Town's three pubs must be one of life's more pleasurable interludes.

NATURAL HISTORY
Along with the rest of the Isles of Scilly, St Mary's is classified as an Area of Outstanding Natural Beauty. Unlike the other more remote islands, much of its interior is intensively farmed for

vegetables and the production of bulbs. However, nature reserves at Porthellick Pool and Lower Moors provide the ideal habitat for waterbirds such as teal, redshank, greenshank and snipe.

Although to a slightly lesser extent than the outer islands, St Mary's still receives a fair number of visiting migrant birds during early spring and autumn. In the south, Old Town Bay and Peninnis Head are regularly visited by many rare species, ranging from warbler and wagtail to pipit and bunting.

HOW TO GET THERE
By air Regular Skybus flights to St Mary's operate from Southampton, Bristol, Exeter, Newquay and Land's End. For details contact Isle of Scilly Travel (tel. 0845 710 5555) or visit their website: www.ios-travel.co.uk
By helicopter Regular flights operate from Penzance to St Mary's. For details contact British International (tel. (01736 363871) or visit their website: www.islesofscillyhelicopter.com
By sea Between April and November, the *Scillonian III* operates a regular passenger ferry service from Penzance to St Mary's. For details contact Isle of Scilly Travel (tel. 0845 710 5555) or visit their website: www.ios-travel.co.uk

ORDNANCE SURVEY MAPS
Landranger 1:50,000 series No. 203

TOURIST INFORMATION
Isles of Scilly Tourist Information Centre, Hugh Town, St Mary's, Isles of Scilly TR21 0LL (tel. 01720 422536). Website: www.simplyscilly.co.uk

WHERE TO STAY
There is a wide range of accommodation on St Mary's, including hotels, bed and breakfast and self-catering facilities, and a campsite. For details contact the Isles of Scilly Tourist Information Centre.

ISLAND WALKS
Unlike the other islands of the Scillies, there are roads and traffic on St Mary's! The best way to explore the island on

Right *The present church at Old Town was built in the 19th century on the site of an older, 12th century building. Its beautiful churchyard not only contains the graves of many shipwrecked souls, but also that of former Prime Minister Harold Wilson who once had a holiday home on the island. St Mary's small airport can be seen in the distance on Salakee Down.*

foot is along the coastal path, a distance of just over eight miles. For a shorter, circular walk, follow the coastal path in an anti-clockwise direction from Hugh Town harbour to The Garrison and Woolpack Point before returning to Hugh Town at Porth Cressa.

There are also two nature trails: Lower Moors between Old Town and Rose Hill; and Higher Moors between Holy Vale and Porth Hellick.

PLACES TO VISIT
● The Garrison
● Woolpack Battery

Above *The entrance gate to the 16th century Star Castle and The Garrison is located a short distance uphill from Hugh Town harbour. By the end of the 19th century, this little peninsula of land had been turned into a heavily armed and fortified stronghold.*

● Mount Flagon and Harry's Walls
● Granite outcrops on Peninnis Head
● Halangy Down Bronze Age chambered tomb and Iron Age village
● The Giant's Tomb on Porth Hellick Down – Bronze Age chambered tomb
● Innisidgen Stone Age chambered tombs

ST AGNES

AND GUGH

The most southwesterly in Britain, the unspoilt islands of St Agnes and its neighbour, Gugh, are the least populated of the Isles of Scilly. Although only three miles in circumference, St Agnes' rugged coastline, rocky coves, white sandy beaches and clear seas offer perfect peace and seclusion for today's visitor. Above all, the island is renowned for the rare migrant birds that take rest here in the late autumn.

ISLES OF SCILLY

Bryher · St Martin's
Atlantic · Tresco
Ocean · Samson
St Agnes · St Mary's
Annet
Bishop Rock · Gugh

St Mary's Sound

Burnt Island
Causeways at low tide
Lighthouse
Church
GUGH
Turks Head
Maze
ST AGNES
Smith Sound
Wingletang Bay
Horse Point

| 0 | kilometres | 2 |
| 0 | mile | 1 |

HISTORY

St Agnes and its little neighbour, Gugh, are the smallest and most southwesterly of the inhabited granite islands of the Isles of Scilly. Until only a few thousand years ago, these two islands and their westerly neighbour, Annet, formed one larger island. Since then, rising sea levels have formed the separate islands that we know today.

Although archæological remains dating from the Late Stone Age have been found on the Isles of Scilly, it was probably not until the Bronze Age (1500–500BC) that they became permanently occupied by farmers and

fishermen. Several chambered tombs and a standing stone from this period can be seen today on the northeast side of Gugh. On St Agnes, St Warna's Well dates from the Iron Age, when pagan Celts lived on these islands. Together with the rest of the Isles of Scilly, St Agnes and Gugh have had many absentee landlords over the centuries and are now administered by the Duchy of Cornwall. Until the recent advent of tourism, life on St Agnes had always centred around farming and fishing. However, the poverty of the islanders during the early 19th century led to many leaving for the mainland and a subsequent decline in the population – in 1841 the population of St Agnes was 243, but by 2001 it had shrunk to 73.

For centuries, the seas around St Agnes had been a graveyard for mariners, and many islanders used to supplement their meagre income by salvaging the contents of wrecked ships. Probably the

Left *Never far from the sea, the sheltered cottage gardens in the centre of St Agnes offer a wonderful view across The Cove towards Gugh. With only two houses, the island of Gugh is the least populated in the Scillies.*

most famous shipwreck off St Agnes was in 1707 when *HMS Firebrand*, one of 21 British men o' war led by Admiral Sir Cloudsley Shovell, foundered in Smith Sound. Some men were able to scramble to safety on the rocks but it is estimated that at least 300 perished in the wreck.

A prominent man-made feature on St Agnes is the old lighthouse in the centre of the island. One of the oldest in England, it was built in 1680 but was replaced in 1911 by a new lighthouse at Penninis Head, on St Mary's.

During the 19th century, the export of early cut flowers to the mainland certainly helped to boost the local economy. Today, however, employment on St Agnes, along with the other islands in the Scilly group, depends mainly on tourism. During the tourist season, which stretches from April to October, visitor numbers are considerably boosted by the thousands of birdwatchers who are attracted to the islands to catch a glimpse of rare migrant birds. St Agnes, in particular, is a favourite destination for 'twitchers', especially during October when the island is often visited by rare birds blown off course from as far away as North America and Siberia.

Above *Overlooked by the omnipresent old lighthouse in the centre of the island, Wingletang Down is littered with large granite boulders. Managed by the Isles of Scilly Wildlife Trust, the heathland is an important site for many species of rare butterflies and plants, including the small adder's-tongue fern.*

NATURAL HISTORY
St Agnes, along with the rest of the Scillies, is classified as an Area of Outstanding Natural Beauty. Although only three miles in circumference, the island's coastline, which contains many sheltered bays, white sandy beaches and rock pools, teems with birdlife. Home to seal and dolphin, the clear waters also support coral, kelp and seagrasss. On the west coast of St Agnes, gigantic granite outcrops, fantastically sculpted by the wind and sea, stand like prehistoric sentries overlooking the ocean.

Strewn with granite boulders, the downland areas, such as Wingletang Down on St Agnes and also on Gugh, are important sites for many rare insects, butterflies and plants and are managed by the Isles of Scilly Wildlife Trust (website: www.ios-wildlifetrust.org.uk).

Above *The slipway of the old lifeboat station at Lower Town overlooks Blanket Bay towards Burnt Island. This little island, which can be reached on foot at low tide, features a stone day mark, or navigational aid, for shipping.*

Below *Shaped by the wind and sea, giant granite outcrops, or carns, are a feature of the island's south and west coasts. Here, at Castle Vean, nature's masterpieces of sculpture tower over more recent, man-made, examples.*

Ablaze with the colour of wildflowers during the spring and early summer, St Agnes is also famed for its birdlife. During October, the island is visited by rare birds blown off course from as far away as North America and Siberia. Species recently sighted on St Agnes include the short-toed eagle,. little bustard and cream-coloured courser.

HOW TO GET THERE

By air Regular Skybus flights to St Mary's operate from Southampton, Bristol, Exeter, Newquay and Land's End. For details contact Isle of Scilly Travel (tel. 0845 710 5555) or visit their website: www.ios-travel.co.uk

By helicopter Regular flights operate from Penzance to St Mary's. For details contact British International (tel. 01736 363871) or visit their website: www.islesofscillyhelicopter.com From St Mary's airport, visitors are conveyed by bus or taxi to Hugh Town harbour to connect with the boat service to St Agnes.

By sea Between April and November, the *Scillonian III* operates a regular passenger ferry service from Penzance to St Mary's. For details contact Isle of Scilly Travel (tel. 0845 710 5555) or visit their website: www.ios-travel.co.uk A boat service to St Agnes operates from Hugh Town harbour on St Mary's.

ORDNANCE SURVEY MAPS

Landranger 1:50,000 series No. 203

TOURIST INFORMATION

Isles of Scilly Tourist Information Centre, Hugh Town, St Mary's, Isles of Scilly TR21 0LL (tel. 01720 422536). Website: www.simplyscilly.co.uk

WHERE TO STAY

Accommodation is limited to a few bed and breakfast and self-catering establishments, and a campsite. For details contact the Isles of Scilly Tourist Information Centre (see above).

ISLAND WALKS

St Agnes is virtually traffic-free. A three-mile circular footpath around the island's coastline offers spectacular views out to the Western Rocks and the Bishop Rock lighthouse. At low tide it is possible to cross on foot to the island of Gugh, where a circular coastal path takes in several Bronze Age sites and extensive views across St Mary's Sound.

PLACES TO VISIT

● Troy Town Maze
● Turk's Head – the most southwesterly pub in Britain
● St Warna's Well
● Bronze Age chambered tombs on the island of Gugh (reached on foot over a sand bar at low tide)

TROY TOWN MAZE

This small turf and pebble maze, laid out in a sunwise direction, is located on the west coast of St Agnes at Camper Dizzle Point, and its origins are shrouded in the mists of time. Because of its similarities to turf mazes found elsewhere in Europe, some believe that it was built by the Vikings when they landed here in the 9th or 10th centuries. However, it may just have been built by a bored lighthouse keeper from St Agnes in the 19th century!

Below *The coastline of St Agnes contains many white, sandy beaches. One of the finest is at Periglis on the west coast near Lower Town. Early Christians are thought to have built a chapel near here and the present church, overlooking this beautiful bay, was built in 1845 with the proceeds from a salvaged wreck.*

TRESCO

Once the lair of pirates and the last bastion of Royalist support during the English Civil War, Tresco and its poverty-stricken population were transformed in 1834 when the island, along with the rest of the Scillies, was leased from the Duchy of Cornwall by Augustus Smith. Since then, Smith and his descendants, the Dorrien–Smith family, have left an indelible mark on this beautiful island. Today, Tresco, with its world-famous Abbey Gardens and unspoilt white, sandy beaches, is the most popular destination for visitors to the Isles of Scilly.

This exotic King Protea (protea cynaroides), a native of South Africa, is one of the many sub-tropical plants that can be seen in the famous Tresco Abbey Gardens.

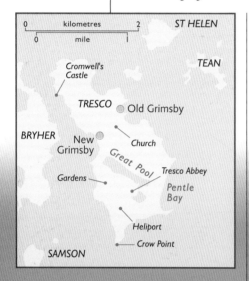

ISLES OF SCILLY

Bryher · St Martin's
Atlantic Ocean · Tresco
Samson
St Agnes · St Mary's
Annet · Gugh
Bishop Rock

ST HELEN

kilometres 2
mile 1

TEAN

Cromwell's Castle

TRESCO · Old Grimsby

BRYHER · New Grimsby · Church
Great Pool
Gardens · Tresco Abbey
Pentle Bay

Heliport
Crow Point
SAMSON

Below *On Tresco's east coast, the white, sandy beaches of Pentle Bay offer a perfect escape from modern life. In the distance is the island of St Martin's.*

HISTORY

Until only a few thousand years ago, Tresco and its near neighbours together formed a much larger island known as Ennor. Since then, rising sea levels have formed the islands that we know today. However, during the very low spring tides, it is still possible to wade across from Tresco to Bryher.

Although archæological remains dating from the Late Stone Age have been found on the Isles of Scilly, it was probably not until the Bronze Age (1500–500BC) that they became permanently occupied by farmers and fishermen. A chambered tomb from this period can be seen today on the summit of Tregarthen Hill in the rugged northern part of Tresco. To the south, remains of Iron Age field boundary walls and hut circles can clearly be seen during low tide at Pentle Bay and Bathinghouse Porth. It is also likely that the Romans traded with the islanders, as coins dating from the period of their occupation of Britain have been found at several locations in the Scillies.

In 1120, a Benedictine priory was founded on the island and, along with the rest of the Isles of Scilly, Tresco was granted to Tavistock Abbey by Henry I. A ruined archway from the priory can be seen today standing in the grounds of the Abbey Gardens.

Although the monks lived peacefully on Tresco until the 16th century, the island, with its sheltered and secluded anchorage of New Grimsby Harbour, also attracted pirates, as an excellent base for their forays against shipping. Although efforts were made to put an end to this anarchy – over 100 pirates were beheaded on the island in a single day in 1209 – pirates continued to operate out of Tresco until the 17th century.

During the English Civil War, the Isles of Scilly became the last Royalist stronghold in the country. Led by Admiral Blake, a Parliamentarian fleet finally took back the islands in 1651 – three years after the war had ended on the mainland! Both Cromwell's Castle, north of New Grimsby, and Oliver's Battery, near Old Grimsby, were built

about this time to protect Tresco against possible attack by the Dutch navy.

After centuries of anarchy and war, life for the people of Tresco had become increasingly difficult and, by the 18th century, there was a great deal of poverty on the island. Tired of scratching a living from farming, fishing, smuggling and shipwrecks, many islanders left for the mainland and the population dropped from 430 in 1841 to 266 in 1871. In 1834 their absentee landlords, the Duchy of Cornwall, agreed to lease the Isles of Scilly to Augustus Smith, a wealthy

banker from Berkhamsted, Hertfordshire.

A keen supporter of public rights, Smith had also championed education for poor children in his home town. On Tresco, where he lived from 1853 until his death in 1872, and on the other islands, he continued his good works, building schools, introducing compulsory education and new agricultural methods and generally raising the islanders' living standards. Augustus Smith also started the building of the modern Abbey on Tresco, using stone from the ruined priory, and created the now world-famous sub-

Above *New Grimsby, with its rows of self-catering cottages, sandy beach, fishing boats and harbour is the main departure and entry point for visitors travelling to Tresco by boat.*

tropical Abbey Gardens. On his death, Smith was succeeded by his nephew Captain Thomas Dorrien-Smith, who continued to enlarge the Abbey and Gardens, introduced the cut-flower industry to the island, and developed tourism. Succeeding members of the Dorrien-Smith family have continued to leave their individual mark on Tresco,

culminating in 1973 when the present owner, Robert Dorrien-Smith, opened a heliport next to the Abbey Gardens.

During both World Wars, Tresco was a base for flying boats protecting Atlantic convoys from U-boat attack. Remains of the slipway can be seen today on Farm Beach near the Estate Office. During World War II, the island was also a base for top secret clandestine operations against the Germans in Occupied France. Using specially converted Breton fishing boats, agents sailed from Tresco to Brittany to gain vital information on German defences in preparation for the Allied landings on D-Day.

Now the most popular destination within the Isles of Scilly, Tresco attracts thousands of visitors each year. With direct helicopter flights from the mainland, major attractions such as the Abbey and Gardens and as a mecca for birdwatchers and botanists, the island can be busy during the high season. It is always possible, however, to find peace and solitude on the beautiful, white sandy beaches of the east coast.

Below *New Grimsby Harbour is a sheltered stretch of water separating Tresco from Bryher. Cromwell's Castle, standing on a small promontory in the distance, was built during the 17th century to protect the harbour from attack by the Dutch navy.*

NATURAL HISTORY

Tresco, along with the rest of the Scillies, is classified as an Area of Outstanding Natural Beauty. For an island only two miles in length and under a mile wide, Tresco contains a wide range of habitats that support numerous species of wild plant, insect and bird, and, due to its extreme southwesterly location, has become a focal point not only for migrating birds but also for many rare species of butterfly and moth.

In the treeless north, the rugged coastline, granite outcrops and open moorland offer the ideal habitat for seabirds and birds of prey and is an ideal place to see kittiwake, fulmar, golden plover, northern wheatear and merlin.

The centre of the island is marked by tall hedgerows that surround the small bulb fields where migrant warbler, pipit and wagtail can be seen in spring. During early summer, the quiet byways and hedgerows abound with wild flowers, including wall oxalis, dark wood violet, three-cornered leek, red campion and foxglove.

South of the agricultural heart of Tresco lie Great Pool and the adjoining, smaller, Abbey Pool. The reedbeds and shallows surrounding these two pools are important nesting sites for many species of waterbird, such as grey heron, little egret and water rail.

South of Great Pool, the Abbey Gardens contain thousands of rare and exotic sub-tropical plant species collected by the Dorrien-Smith family over the last 150 years from around the world. The internationally-famous gardens, protected from the prevailing winds by a wall of trees planted by Augustus Smith in the mid-19th century, are at their best in spring and early summer.

Finally, the long, white sandy beaches, sand flats and dunes of the south and southeast coast of Tresco are a haven for many birds including turnstone, curlew, whimbrel and oystercatcher, while offshore sandwich tern and shag can be seen feeding in the clear blue waters.

HOW TO GET THERE

By air Regular Skybus flights to St Mary's operate from Southampton, Bristol, Exeter, Newquay and Land's End. For details contact Isle of Scilly Travel (tel. 0845 710 5555) or visit their website: www.ios-travel.co.uk
From St Mary's airport, visitors are conveyed by bus or taxi to Hugh Town harbour to connect with the boat service to Tresco.
By helicopter Regular direct flights operate from Penzance to Tresco. For details contact British International (tel. 01736 363871) or visit their website: www.islesofscillyhelicopter.com

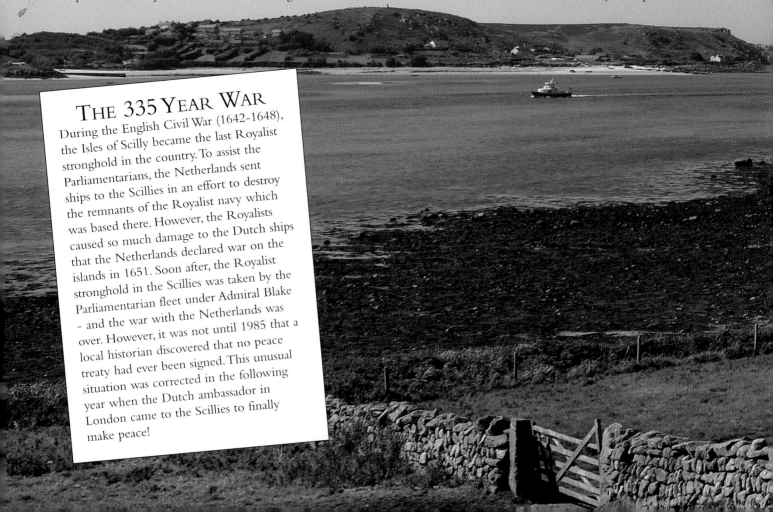

THE 335 YEAR WAR
During the English Civil War (1642-1648), the Isles of Scilly became the last Royalist stronghold in the country. To assist the Parliamentarians, the Netherlands sent ships to the Scillies in an effort to destroy the remnants of the Royalist navy which was based there. However, the Royalists caused so much damage to the Dutch ships that the Netherlands declared war on the islands in 1651. Soon after, the Royalist stronghold in the Scillies was taken by the Parliamentarian fleet under Admiral Blake – and the war with the Netherlands was over. However, it was not until 1985 that a local historian discovered that no peace treaty had ever been signed. This unusual situation was corrected in the following year when the Dutch ambassador in London came to the Scillies to finally make peace!

Right *Tresco was a windswept, treeless island until Augustus Smith leased it from the Duchy of Cornwall in 1834. By planting hundreds of trees to form windbreaks, Smith and succeeding members of his family established the world-famous Abbey Gardens. This important and unique collection contains many thousands of species of sub-tropical trees and plants from the southern hemisphere.*

By sea Between April and November, the *Scillonian III* operates a regular passenger ferry service from Penzance to St Mary's. For details contact Isle of Scilly Travel (tel. 0845 710 5555) or visit their website: www.ios-travel.co.uk
A boat service to Tresco operates from Hugh Town harbour on St Mary's.

ORDNANCE SURVEY MAPS
Landranger 1:50,000 series No. 203

TOURIST INFORMATION
Isles of Scilly Tourist Information Centre, Hugh Town, St Mary's, Isles of Scilly TR21 0LL (tel. 01720 422536).
Website: www.simplyscilly.co.uk
or visit Tresco's own website: www.tresco.co.uk

WHERE TO STAY
There is a good range of accommodation on Tresco, from the luxurious Island Hotel and the New Inn to a wide choice of self-catering properties. For further details either contact the Isles of Scilly

Information Centre (see above) or visit Tresco's own website: www.tresco.co.uk
There is no campsite on Tresco.

ISLAND WALKS
Apart from a few tractors and electric buggies, Tresco is traffic-free. From the quay at New Grimsby, a footpath heads northwest along the coastline to the rugged northern end of the island where there are magnificent views across to Bryher. Turning southeast, the path continues to the sandy beaches and dunes of the southern end before heading north back to New Grimsby. From the east coast are panoramic views across to

St Martin's. A full circular walk round Tresco is about five miles in length and there are many opportunities to take short cuts across the island via the world famous Tresco Abbey Gardens.

PLACES TO VISIT
- Tresco Abbey Gardens
- Valhalla Museum
- Great Pool and Abbey Pool
- New Inn pub
- St Nicholas Church
- Cromwell's Castle
- King Charles' Castle
- 16th century blockhouse

BRYHER

R ugged and beautiful, the granite mass of the island of Bryher is lashed by Atlantic storms in winter and kissed by the sun in summer. For centuries a graveyard for many an unsuspecting ship, the island's wild west coast is today a favourite haunt for birdwatchers. After 5,000 years of human habitation, this unspoilt island is now the perfect destination for visitors wishing to escape the stresses and strains of modern life.

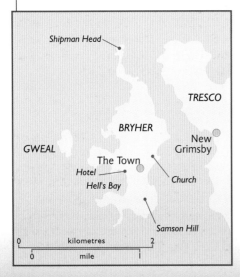

ISLES OF SCILLY

Below *The rocks and islets around Bryher's west coast have for centuries been a graveyard for ships. In 1910, the Atlantic Transport's 13,443-ton steamship* Minnehaha, *en route from London to New York, ran aground in fog on Scilly Rock just to the west of the island. Subsequently refloated and repaired, she was torpedoed by a German submarine in 1917.*

HISTORY

The history of Bryher, the smallest of the inhabited Isles of Scilly, is closely linked with its larger neighbour, Tresco (see pages 46-47), to which it was physically joined until the 16th century. Inhabited for at least the last 5,000 years, Bryher contains numerous prehistoric sites, including over 100 burial cairns on Shipman Head Down at the north of the island, chambered tombs on Samson Hill, ancient field boundary walls seen at low tide in Green Bay and hut circles and field systems around Heathy Hill.

During the English Civil War, the Isles of Scilly became the last Royalist stronghold in the country. Led by Admiral Blake, a Parliamentarian fleet finally took back the islands in 1651 – three years after the war had ended on the mainland! In addition to the fortifications built on Tresco, several gun batteries were built on the east coast of

Bryher to protect New Grimsby Harbour against possible attack by the Dutch navy. Little remains of these batteries today, but the keen eye can still see earthworks along Works Point and along The Green. The ruins of a watch house can also be found on Watch Hill. In the narrow channel of New Grimsby Harbour, Hangman's Island, with its replica gibbet, is a local landmark. It was here that Admiral Blake hung mutinous Royalist sailors during the Civil War.

Over the following centuries, the small population of Bryher scratched a living from farming, fishing, kelp burning, piloting, flower growing and a spot of smuggling. During the 18th century, kelp burning was developed into an important industry throughout the Isles of Scilly. The soda and potash extracted from burnt. dried seaweed were important ingredients used in the

SAMSON

After scratching a living from farming the last inhabitants left the twin-peaked and treeless island of Samson in 1855. Their roofless houses on the lower slopes of South Hill, as well as prehistoric chambered cairns and a field system on North Hill, can be seen by visitors to the island today. Boat trips to Samson are run during the summer months from Hugh Town harbour on St Mary's.

Above *In contrast to Bryher's rugged west coast, its sheltered east coast contains secluded, sandy beaches with views across to Tresco.*

manufacture of glass and soap on the mainland. Remains of a stone-lined kelp pit can be seen on Bryher today close to the shoreline north of Heathy Hill.

Today, apart from its small boatbuilding industry and a few local fishermen, Bryher caters solely for visitors eager to escape the hustle and bustle of modern life.

NATURAL HISTORY

In late spring and early summer, Bryher is ablaze with colour, not only from bright yellow gorse but also from the many wildflowers that grow on this unspoilt island. A favourite haunt for birdwatchers, Bryher's west coast attracts many seabirds including black-backed and herring gull, gannet, kittiwake and skua. Offshore, the Northern Rocks are home to breeding puffin, shag, cormorant, razorbill and guillemot. During the summer, the gorse-covered hillsides of Bryher are a favourite haunt for linnet, cuckoo and stonechat. Native birds include wren, robin and finch and, during the autumn, rare migratory birds from as far afield as Asia and North Americas are also regularly seen here.

HOW TO GET THERE

By air Regular Skybus flights to St Mary's operate from Southampton, Bristol, Exeter, Newquay and Land's End. For details contact Isle of Scilly Travel (tel. 0845 710 5555) or visit their website: www.ios-travel.co.uk From St Mary's airport, visitors are conveyed by bus or taxi to Hugh Town harbour to connect with the boat service to Bryher.

By helicopter Regular flights operate from Penzance to St Mary's. For details contact British International (tel. 01736 363871) or visit their website: www.islesofscillyhelicopter.com From St Mary's airport, visitors are conveyed by bus or taxi to Hugh Town harbour to connect with the boat service to Bryher.

By sea Between April and November, the *Scillonian III* operates a regular passenger ferry service from Penzance to St Mary's. For details contact Isle of Scilly Travel (tel. 0845 710 5555) or visit their website: www.ios-travel.co.uk A boat service to Bryher operates from Hugh Town harbour on St Mary's.

ORDNANCE SURVEY MAPS

Landranger 1:50,000 series No. 203

TOURIST INFORMATION

Isles of Scilly Tourist Information Centre, Hugh Town, St Mary's, Isles of Scilly TR21 0LL (tel. 01720 422536). Website: www.simplyscilly.co.uk

WHERE TO STAY

There are two guest houses, five self-catering properties and one campsite on Bryher. For more details contact the Isles of Scilly Information Centre (see above) or visit Bryher's website: www.bryher-ios.co.uk The Hell Bay Hotel (tel. 01720 422947) offers comfortable accommodation set on the dramatic west coast of the island. For more details visit the website: www.tresco.co.uk

ISLAND WALKS

Apart from a few local vehicles, Bryher is virtually traffic-free. From either of the two quays on Bryher - Church Quay for high water and the newer Anneka's Quay for low water - a four mile footpath traverses the entire coastline and offers dramatic views along the exposed and rugged west coast and also across New Grimsby Harbour to Tresco. This route can be varied or shortened by taking the road across the centre of the island.

PLACES TO VISIT

● 18th century church of All Saints
● Prehistoric burial cairns on Shipman Down, chambered tomb on Samson Hill

ST MARTIN'S

Renowned for its deserted sandy beaches and unpolluted blue sea, St Martin's is the third largest island of the Isles of Scilly. Commercial flower and bulb growing for export, introduced in the 19th century, has now been overtaken by tourism as the island's most important economic activity. Today, unspoilt by unfettered modern commercialisation, St Martin's offers a unique island experience for those seeking peace and solitude.

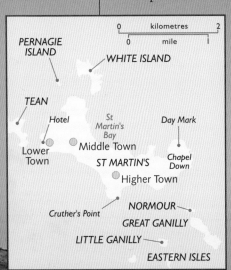

ISLES OF SCILLY

Bryher · St Martin's · Atlantic Ocean · Tresco · Samson · St Agnes · Annet · St Mary's · Gugh · Bishop Rock

PERNAGIE ISLAND · WHITE ISLAND · TEAN · Hotel · St Martin's Bay · Day Mark · Lower Town · Middle Town · ST MARTIN'S · Chapel Down · Higher Town · Cruther's Point · NORMOUR · GREAT GANILLY · LITTLE GANILLY · EASTERN ISLES

kilometres   0 — 2
mile   0 — 1

Above *This red and white Day Mark on Chapel Down was built of granite in 1687 as a mark for shipping. Ruined buildings nearby are all that remain of a signal station built during the Napoleonic wars.*

HISTORY

Until only a few thousand years ago St Martin's, along with the islands of Tresco, Bryher and St Mary's, together formed a much larger island known as Ennor. Since then, rising sea levels have formed the islands that we know today. Although archæological remains dating from the Late Stone Age have been found on the Isles of Scilly, it was probably not until the Bronze Age (1500-500BC) that they became permanently occupied by farmers and fishermen. Much of the evidence from this period now lies beneath the sea, but there are still several important sites that can be seen today on St Martin's. Several burial chambers can be found on Cruther's Hill in the south, and on Chapel Down in the northeast. Artefacts such as coins, pottery and jewellery, found on the nearby uninhabited island of Nornour, also suggest that Roman traders visited the

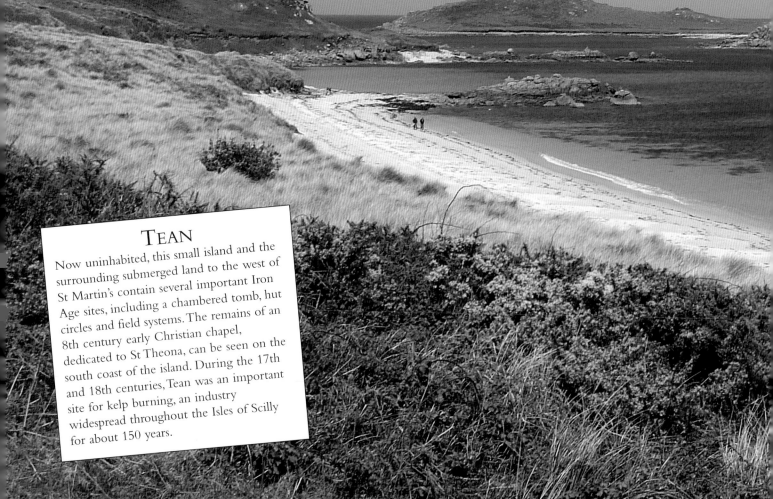

TEAN

Now uninhabited, this small island and the surrounding submerged land to the west of St Martin's contain several important Iron Age sites, including a chambered tomb, hut circles and field systems. The remains of an 8th century early Christian chapel, dedicated to St Theona, can be seen on the south coast of the island. During the 17th and 18th centuries, Tean was an important site for kelp burning, an industry widespread throughout the Isles of Scilly for about 150 years.

islands, although there is no evidence of any permanent settlement. Christianity came to St Martin's in the late 5th century and remains of a chapel from this period can be seen on Chapel Down.

Not much is known of life on the island until the 17th century, when it is thought that about 70 people were living there. Mainly poor farmers and fishermen, their quiet life was rudely disturbed during the English Civil War when Parliamentarian forces under Admiral Blake retook the islands, hung many local Royalists and destroyed many of the island's farms. St Martin's church was built in 1683 and subsequently rebuilt in 1866, after being struck by lightning. The red and white Day Mark which dominates the island on Chapel Down was built of granite in 1687 as a beacon for shipping. About this time, kelp burning was introduced to St Martin's and gave employment to the island's people for the next 150 years. The soda ash that was produced was exported to the mainland for the glass trade.

After a visit to the Isles of Scilly by John Wesley in 1743, Methodist chapels were built on the islands. On St Martin's, a dissenting chapel was subsequently built in 1845 at Higher Town and is still in use with regular weekly services.

In 1834, the Duchy of Cornwall agreed to lease the Isles of Scilly to Augustus Smith, a wealthy banker from Berkhamsted, Hertfordshire (see pages 47-48). He not only introduced modern farming methods to the islands, but also the flower industry. On St Martin's this was of great importance, as other industries such as piloting, boat-building and the early potato harvest were all failing. By the early 20th century, there were 20 flower farms on the island providing employment for many of the islanders. However, life was still not easy for them. Living conditions were poor, hours were long and the work was hard. The remains of large steam heated glasshouses and packing sheds can still be seen on the island's farms, a few of which still produce flowers and bulbs for export.

By the 1920s St Martin's, with its numerous unspoilt sandy beaches and crystal clear waters, was being recognised as a holiday destination, and from then the island's tourist industry has developed to its present level of importance.

BULB FIELDS

Flowers and bulbs are still grown commercially on St Martin's. The small sheltered fields, with their high hedgerows of euonymus or pittosporum in the south of the island, offer perfect growing conditions not only for many species of daffodil but also for exotic plants such as *amaryllis belladonna*.

Below *On the north coast of the island is the beautiful sweep of St Martin's Bay. Its white sandy beach and turquoise waters are totally unspoilt and, even during the peak holiday season, remain uncrowded.*

NATURAL HISTORY

St Martin's, along with the rest of the Isles of Scilly, is classified as an Area of Outstanding Natural Beauty. A paradise for ornithologists in the autumn. the island is ideally situated for migrant birds from the Continent and as far away as North America and Asia. During the breeding season, the northern and eastern coasts of St Martin's, and outer islands such as Men-a-vaur, are home to large colonies of guillemot, fulmar and razorbill. To the east, the small uninhabited islands of Nornour, Ganilly and Arthur support large colonies of shag, cormorant and Atlantic grey seal. At low tide, large numbers of dunlin, sanderling, grey and ringed plover frequent the open sandflats to the south of the island.

St Martin's sheltered south facing coast provides ideal growing conditions for both wild and cultivated flowers. In early summer, the hedgerows on this side of the island are covered with wild agapanthus, lily, tree mallow and hotentot fig, while the more exposed north coast is ablaze with bright yellow gorse.

HOW TO GET THERE

By air Regular Skybus flights to St Mary's operate from Southampton, Bristol, Exeter, Newquay and Land's End. For details contact Isle of Scilly Travel (tel. 0845 710 5555) or visit their website: www.ios-travel.co.uk

By helicopter Regular direct flights operate from Penzance to St Mary's. For details contact British International (tel. 01736 363871) or visit their website: www.islesofscillyhelicopter.com

From St Mary's airport, visitors are conveyed by bus or taxi to Hugh Town harbour to connect with the boat service to St Martin's.

By sea Between April and November, the *Scillonian III* operates a regular passenger ferry service from Penzance to St Mary's. For details contact Isle of Scilly Travel (tel. 0845 710 5555) or visit their website: www.ios-travel.co.uk

A boat service to St Martin's operates from Hugh Town harbour on St Mary's.

ORDNANCE SURVEY MAPS

Landranger 1:50,000 series No. 203

TOURIST INFORMATION

Isles of Scilly Tourist Information Centre, Hugh Town, St Mary's, Isles of Scilly TR21 0LL (tel. 01720 422536). Website: www.simplyscilly.co.uk

WHERE TO STAY

There is a small range of accommodation on St Martin's, from the luxurious St Martin's Hotel to two guest houses, eight self-catering cottages and a campsite. For further details contact the Isles of Scilly Tourist Information Centre (see above).

ISLAND WALKS

Apart from a few local vehicles, St Martin's is virtually traffic-free. From either of the two quays on the island –

ST HELEN'S

This small unihabited island to the northwest of Tean (see page 52) contains the remains of an 8th century early Christian chapel, dedicated to St Elidius, and a hermit's cell. The feast day of St Elidius is still celebrated on the island on 6th August each year. The ruins of an 18th century isolation hospital can also be seen on the south of the island. To the north of St Helen's, the lighthouse on Round Island was built in 1887, and automated in 1987.

Higher Town Quay for high water and Lower Town Quay for low water – a six mile footpath traverses much of the coastline and offers dramatic views across to Tresco and the Eastern Isles. This route can be varied or shortened by taking several tracks that criss-cross the island or along the spine road that runs from Lower Town to Higher Town.

PLACES TO VISIT
● Sevenstones Inn
● Day Mark and signal station on Chapel Down
● St Martin's Vineyard
● North Farm Gallery
● St Martin's Church
● Craft bakery
● Bronze Age burial chambers on Cruthers Hill

Right *The colourful and beautifully tended gardens of the residents of Higher Town offer them breathtaking views across the bay to the uninhabited Eastern Isles.*

Above *Of all of the Isles of Scilly, St Martin's possesses some of the finest beaches in England. Here, the curving sands of Higher Town Bay offer perfect peace and solitude for the discerning traveller.*

ST MICHAEL'S MOUNT

D uring Roman times, St Michael's Mount was the principle harbour for the export of Cornish tin to the Mediterranean. In 1144, a monastery was founded by French monks from Mont St Michel and the island became a place of prayer, meditation and pilgrimage.

After suffering earthquake, plague, rebellious incursions and siege, the island was bought by the St Aubyn family in 1659 and remained in their ownership until it was given to the National Trust in 1954.

Today, it is one of the most popular tourist destinations in Cornwall.

CORNWALL

A30

A394

Penzance

Marazion

Tidal causeway

Priory

Mount's Bay

ST MICHAEL'S MOUNT

kilometres 2

mile 1

HISTORY

St Michael's Mount became an island about 2,000 years ago, when rising sea levels flooded what is now Mount's Bay. During Roman times, Cornish tin was in high demand and much of it was exported to the Mediterranean from the island's harbour. From the 6th century, early Christian monks probably used the island as a place for prayer and meditation.

The history of St Michael's Mount becomes much clearer following the Norman invasion of England in 1066. Following the invasion, William the Conqueror gave large areas of land in Cornwall to Robert, the Count of Mortain. In turn, Robert granted the island to the Abbot of Mont St Michel in northern France. By the 12th century, he had built a small monastery on the island dedicated to St Michael, and it is from this date that the

island received its name.

Over the next 200 years, the monks of St Michael's Mount not only suffered from an earthquake and the plague but also, during war with France, were treated suspiciously because of their allegiance to the Abbot of Mont St Michel. In 1424, St Michael's Mount was given by Henry VI to the Abbess of the newly founded Syon Abbey at Twickenham. Now in English hands, the monastery on the island was expanded and a new harbour constructed to shelter ships entering Mount's Bay. Income for the monastery came from dues levied on all ships using the harbour.

Until the Dissolution of the Monasteries in 1535, when the island and its monastery were seized by the Crown, St Michael's Mount was captured for brief periods on three occasions during times of rebellion – in 1193 by Henry de la Pomeray, in 1473 by the Earl of Oxford and in 1497 by Perkin Warbeck. Later, in 1549, the

Mount was again captured, this time by Roman Catholic Cornish rebels led by Sir Humphrey Arundell.

For a brief period after the Dissolution of the Monasteries, the Mount was leased by the Crown to wealthy Cornish landowners who were obliged to station a small garrison there, but, by the early 17th century, it had been sold to Sir Robert Cecil. In 1640, after becoming the Earl of Salisbury, Cecil sold the island to wealthy Cornish landowner Francis Basset. During the English Civil War Basset, a Royalist supporter, set about improving the castle's defences and turned it into a virtually impregnable fortress. Following their defeat of the Royalists in Cornwall in 1646, Parliamentarian forces laid siege to the Mount but, within a short time, Bassett surrendered and fled to the Isles of Scilly – the last Royalist stronghold in the country. In 1647, John St Aubyn was

appointed military governor of the Mount and later purchased the island. The Mount remained in the ownership of the St Aubyn family until 1954, when it was given to the National Trust.

For over 300 years, the Mount was used as the private residence of the St Aubyn family and, during that time, they rebuilt the harbour, extended the island's village and added the terraced gardens and wings to the seaward side of the castle. During the Napoleonic war against France in the late 18th century, the garrison on St Michael's Mount was strengthened to repel the threatened invasion. The invasion never came, but the guns on the Mount were fired on two occasions against French ships that had sailed into Mount's Bay.

Unseen by visitors is a funicular underground railway, not open to the public, which was opened in 1912 to carry goods from the harbour up to the castle at the top of the Mount.

Although it has been owned by the National Trust since 1954, the descendants of the St Aubyn family still live in the Victorian wing of the castle. Both the castle, church and terraced gardens are open to the public between late March and late October each year.

NATURAL HISTORY

Set in an Area of Outstanding Natural Beauty, St Michael's Mount is visited by thousands of people each year. Best viewed from a boat, its rugged granite cliffs on the west side are a favourite haunt for seabirds, while seals can often be seen basking on the rocks and swimming in the sea. The castle keep is a good vantage point to watch for pods of dolphin that regularly visit the waters of Mount's Bay.

A delight for the botanist, the magnificent walled terraced gardens on the south slopes of St Michael's Mount were laid out during the 18th century. Many of the rare sub-tropical trees and shrubs from the southern hemisphere, including aloe, yucca, strelitzia and giant agave, were planted here by the second Lord St Levan in the early 20th century.

HOW TO GET THERE

At low tide On foot across causeway from Marazion

At high tide A regular ferry service operates to St Michael's Mount from Marazion. For tide and ferry information contact the island office (tel. 01736 710507) or vist their website: www.stmichaelsmount.co.uk

The castle is open between the end of March and the end of October. There are no facilities for dogs on the island.

ORDNANCE SURVEY MAPS

Landranger 1:50,000 series No. 203

TOURIST INFORMATION

Penzance Tourist Information Centre, Station Approach, Penzance TR18 2NF. (tel. 01736 362207)
Website: www.go-cornwall.com

Above *In 1588, a beacon was lit on top of the church on St Michael's Mount to signal the approach of the Spanish Armada. The Victorian wing of the castle, designed by Piers St Aubyn, was completed in 1878.*

WHERE TO STAY

There is a wide range of accommodation in and around Marazion and Penzance on the nearby mainland. For more details contact the Penzance Tourist Information Centre (see above).

ISLAND WALKS

A steep track with rough-hewn steps leads from the National Trust shop near the harbour to the castle, where there are far reaching views across Mount's Bay to Penzance. The track is not suitable for the infirm or disabled. A more level route leads from the harbour to the walled terraced gardens.

Below *At low tide, it is possible to walk across the ancient causeway that links Marazion with St Michael's Mount. At high tide, a regular boat service operates the short distance across to the harbour. During periods of low tide, the boat operates trips around the island from the harbour.*

HMS WARSPITE

Probably the most famous British battleship of the 20th century, *HMS Warspite* (33,410 tons) was launched in 1913 and saw action during World War I in the Battle of Jutland. During World War II she was involved in many engagements with the enemy, including the Second Battle of Narvik (April 1940), the Mediterranean (summer of 1940), the Indian Ocean (1942), the Mediterranean (1943) and the Allied landings in Normandy (June 1944). In 1945, she was placed in reserve and sold for scrap two years later. Affectionately know as 'The Old Lady', *HMS Warspite* ran aground in Mount's Bay next to St Michael's Mount on her way to the breaker's yard in 1950. Firmly stuck on the rocks, she was broken up and salvaged on the beach at Marazion.

LOOE ISLAND

Once a place of worship and devotion, privately-owned Looe Island was for centuries home to a small number of farmers, fishermen and smugglers. With a diverse variety of natural habitats, this small island is now managed by the Cornwall Wildlife Trust as a marine nature reserve. The waters around its coastline, rich in marine life, are now giving important clues in the study of global warming. From Easter to September, visitors to the island can enjoy its peace and tranquility away from the hustle and bustle of the nearby mainland.

Above *Jetty Cottage is one of only three buildings on the island. Visitors to the island are greeted at this information centre by the local warden of the Cornwall Wildlife Trust.*

Below *Between Easter and September a licensed boatman carries visitors on the short journey to Looe Island from the quay at East Looe. A landing charge is collected on arrival.*

HISTORY

Also known as St George's Island, Looe Island has been occupied since the 11th century, when a small chapel was built on its summit. By the 12th century, the island was owned by the Benedictine abbey of Glastonbury. At that time the island could be reached on foot at low tide but since then, rising sea levels have made this impossible. The chapel had become disused by the mid-16th century.

In 1743, the island was bought by Edward Trelawny, a local MP and Governor of Jamaica, and remained as part of the Trelawny estate until 1921. During that time the island was leased to various families, who eked out a living from farming and fishing. In an effort to prevent smuggling, a coastguard was posted on the island from about 1830.

Between 1921 and 1964, ownership of the island changed hands several times until it was bought by the Atkins sisters from Epsom in Surrey. They, in turn, bequeathed the island to the Cornwall Wildlife Trust who now manage it as a Marine Nature Reserve.

NATURAL HISTORY

The 22 acre island is home to a wide variety of habitats including woodland, grassland, cliffs, rocky beach and reefs. Nesting seabirds are attracted to the island including a large colony of great black-backed gull. The surrounding waters are rich in marine life and grey seal, bottlenose dolphin and basking shark can often be seen offshore.

HOW TO GET THERE

From Easter until September there is a boat service to Looe Island from the quay at East Looe. For further information contact Looe Tourist Information Centre (see below) or the Cornwall Wildlife Trust (tel. 01872 273939).
Website: www.cornwallwildlifetrust.org.uk

ORDNANCE SURVEY MAPS

Landranger 1:50,000 series No. 201

TOURIST INFORMATION

Nearest office: The Guildhall, Fore Street, East Looe, Cornwall PL13 1AA (tel. 01503 262072 or 01503 262409).
Website: www.looecornwall.com

WHERE TO STAY

There is no accommodation on Looe Island. For accommodation in Looe contact Looe Tourist Information Centre.

ISLAND WALKS

A circular footpath of about one mile enables visitors to enjoy this small, tranquil island. From the 150ft summit, there are extensive views over Looe Bay.

PLACES TO VISIT

- Site of 12th century chapel on summit
- Jetty Cottage
- Trelawny's Island

Right *A place of peace and tranquility, Looe Island is one of the smallest inhabited islands off the coast of Britain.*

THE ATKINS SISTERS

Ⓒ CORONET

— EVELYN E. ATKINS —

WE BOUGHT AN ISLAND

A funny, original, endearing book for daydreamers and nine-to-fivers everywhere.

Two sisters from Epsom in Surrey, Evelyn Atkins and her sister, Babs, had long dreamed of owning their own island. Their dream came true in 1964 when they purchased Looe Island and set up home there. Evelyn's book, published in 1976, tells the story of their epic struggle to survive and their work in conserving the island's habitat. This work is now continued by the Cornwall Wildlife Trust.

BURGH ISLAND

A former haunt of monks, pirates and smugglers, privately-owned Burgh Island lies only 200 metres from the coast at Bigbury-on-Sea in Devon. The 26-acre tidal island can be reached on foot at low tide or on a unique 'sea tractor' at other times. In 1895, Burgh Island was purchased by the famous Victorian music hall entertainer George Chirgwin, who built a small wooden hotel. Now dominated by the 'Great White Palace' - a recently restored 1930s Art Deco hotel once patronised by famous authors, actors and royalty - the island is also famous for its romantic setting in Bigbury Bay and its 14th century inn.

Above *At high tide, an unusual 'sea tractor' carries visitors the short distance from Bigbury-on-Sea to Burgh Island and its Art Deco hotel. The current tractor was commissioned in 1969 and is the only one of its type in the world.*

HISTORY

Located close to the mouth of the River Avon, Burgh Island and the surrounding South Hams were regularly visited by seafaring traders from the Mediterranean who traded their wares of wine, oils and spices for locally mined tin and iron. In medieval times the island was inhabited by monks, and later became a hideaway for pirates and smugglers. The oldest existing building is the Pilchard Inn which dates back to 1336. It was here that the Prince of Smugglers, Tom Crocker, was finally captured by Customs men in the 18th century.

In 1895, the famous music hall entertainer, George Chirgwin ('The Funniest Man on Earth'), purchased the island. At that time, the only buildings on the island were some fishermen's cottages and the Pilchard Inn. In 1896, Chirgwin built a small wooden hotel on the island which he used as retreat from his fans until his death in 1922. Five years later, Chirgwin's widow sold the island to Archibald Nettlefold of the Guest, Keen & Nettlefold engineering company. He commissioned the architect Matthew Dawson to design a luxury Art Deco hotel. Constructed of steel and concrete, it became known as the 'Great White Palace' and was an instant success with well-heeled clients. From the 1930s through to the 1950s it prospered, and attracted many famous clients, including Agatha Christie, Noel Coward, Amy

Johnson and the then Prince of Wales and Wallis Simpson. During World War II, the hotel was taken over by the Royal Air Force as a convalescent centre.

The hotel fell victim to post-war austerity and closed in 1955. For the next 30 years the hotel was divided into self-catering flats, until the island was purchased by Beatrice and Tony Porter in 1985. They set about restoring the hotel to its former glory and it was reopened in 1988. The current owners bought the island in 2001.

NATURAL HISTORY

Burgh Island's rocky coastline provides shelter and a breeding ground for many types of seabird. In the spring and autumn, pods of dolphin can be seen from the island playing in Bigbury Bay.

HOW TO GET THERE

From Bigbury-on-Sea the island can be reached on foot at low tide. At high tide, an unusual sea tractor operated by the hotel provides a ferry service. Parking is available at Bigbury-on-Sea. The hotel has its own heli-pad.

ORDNANCE SURVEY MAP

Landranger 1:50,000 series No. 202

TOURIST INFORMATION

Nearest office: Salcombe Tourist Information Centre, Council Hall, Market Street, Salcombe (tel. 01548 843927).
Website: www.salcombeinformation.co.uk

WHERE TO STAY

Burgh Island Hotel (tel: 01548 810514)
Website: www.burghisland.com

Above *Dating from 1336 and a former haunt of pirates and smugglers, the Pilchard Inn derives its name from the once important local pilchard fishing industry.*

PLACES TO VISIT

● Burgh Island Hotel
● Pilchard Inn

Left *The view of Burgh Island from Bigbury-on-Sea is dominated by its famous 1930s Art Deco hotel - nicknamed the 'Great White Palace'. To the right of it is George Chirgwin's original wooden building.*

Below *The monument to Alfred, Lord Tennyson casts a giant shadow across the chalk downland of Tennyson Down on the Isle of Wight. With their equable climate, natural beauty and rich historical legacy, the islands of Southern England, of which the Isle of Wight is by far the largest, have much to offer the visitor.*

Southern England

Brownsea Island
Isle of Wight
Hayling Island
Thorney Island
Isle of Sheppey

BROWNSEA ISLAND

Once owned by the monks of Cerne Abbey and pillaged by the Vikings, Brownsea Island was chosen by Henry VIII in the 16th century as a site for a castle to protect the entrance to the strategically important Poole Harbour. For the next 400 years, Brownsea attracted many owners, from politicians and an over-ambitious businessman to successful landowners, philanthropic art lovers and finally an eccentric recluse. In 1962, Brownsea Island and its rich diversity of natural habitats was saved for the nation by the National Trust.

Above *In 1852 Colonel William Waugh bought Brownsea Island and erected the neo-Gothic church of St Mary. A later owner of the island, George Cavendish-Bentinck, decorated the church's interior with fine Italian Renaissance sculpture.*

HISTORY

The area around Poole Harbour has been inhabited for at least 2,500 years. Archæological remains have shown that local communities were involved in farming, trading and the making of pottery. Following the Roman occupation, the Anglo-Saxons settled in the region and by 800AD Brownsea Island was part of the Kingdom of Wessex. Ownership of Brownsea then passed to the monks at Cerne Abbey, who built a small chapel on the island.

For the next 200 years, the region was repeatedly attacked by Viking raiding parties, but peace returned after the Norman conquest in 1066. Cerne Abbey continued to own Brownsea and by the 14th century, a small community had been established on the island. Here, life revolved around hunting, fishing and salt-making.

After the Dissolution of the Monasteries in the 16th century, Henry VIII, recognising the strategic importance of Brownsea at the entrance to Poole Harbour, had a small castle, or blockhouse, built on the island. Over the following 200 years, Brownsea had several owners but, by the 18th century, the castle had lost its importance and had become derelict. In 1726, former MP, architect and botanist William Benson bought the island and rebuilt the castle into his grand private house. He also set about preserving the island's plantlife and planted trees. The next owner, Sir Humphrey Sturt, further enlarged the castle and added formal gardens. During the 19th century, an armed coastguard station was built near the castle to guard against smugglers.

In 1852, Colonel William Waugh bought Brownsea and embarked upon a massive development of the island. He built a church, a large pottery and brickworks, a village for his employees, and further extended the castle. Land

was reclaimed from the sea, and the brick wall around it now encloses a large lagoon on the northwest of the island. Within five years, Waugh's ambitious business empire on Brownsea had collapsed and he became bankrupt.

Between 1873 and 1927, Brownsea Island changed hands four more times. In 1896, a major fire destroyed the castle – which was later rebuilt – and, in 1907, Robert Baden-Powell set up the world's first scout camp on the island. It is still used by Scouts and Guides today. By the 1920s, the island had been developed into a successful estate, with vegetable production, dairy farming and daffodil growing supporting a close-knit community.

This all changed in 1927 when the island was sold to Mary Bonham-Christie. An eccentric and reclusive woman, Mary closed down the productive agricultural and horticultural industries and allowed the island to revert back to its natural habitat. The former estate workers left for the mainland, visitors were banned and nature gradually took over.

Brownsea Island slumbered on as a wildlife sanctuary until 1961, when Mary Bonham-Christie died. Fortunately the

National Trust, aided by many generous donors including the John Lewis Partnership, was able to save the island from developers and protect its important habitats. Today, over 100,000 people a year visit Brownsea to enjoy its tranquil woodlands, sheltered beaches and unique wildlife. The Dorset Wildlife Trust leases a large nature reserve at the north of the island, the open-air theatre is now in its 43rd season of Shakespeare plays, and Scouts and Guides from all over the world make their pilgrimage to the birth place of Scouting.

Above *The first Brownsea Castle, a simple blockhouse, was built by Henry VIII in the mid-16th century to guard the entrance to Poole Harbour. It later became a private residence and was elaborately rebuilt by Sir Humphrey Sturt in the 1760s. Today the castle and its grounds are leased from the National Trust by the John Lewis Partnership for use by its employees.*

Below *Visitors to Brownsea land at the quay on the east side of the island. Many of these buildings, including the castellated private pier for the castle and the gatehouse, were built by Colonel William Waugh during the mid-19th century as part of his ill-fated attempt to develop the island.*

Left *The secluded pinewoods of Brownsea Island are home to one of the last surviving colonies of red squirrel in southern England.*

HOW TO GET THERE

The island is open to the public from March until October. During this period, a regular boat service operates to Brownsea from Poole Quay and from Sandbanks. Other services operate from Bournemouth Pier and Swanage. No dogs are allowed on the island. For full details on visiting Brownsea Island contact The National Trust office on the island (tel. 01202 707744) or visit www.nationaltrust.org.uk/brownsea

ORDNANCE SURVEY MAPS

Landranger 1:50,000 series No. 195

TOURIST INFORMATION

Poole Tourism, Enefco House, Poole Quay, Poole, Dorset BH15 1HJ (tel. 01202 253253). Website: www.pooletourism.com

WHERE TO STAY

A wide variety of accommodation, from caravan and camping sites to hotels, is available in the Poole area. For more information contact Poole Tourist Information Centre.

For holiday accommodation on Brownsea Island contact National Trust Holiday Cottages (tel. 0870 4584422). Website: www.nationaltrustcottages.co.uk

NATURAL HISTORY

For its small size, Brownsea Island contains an amazingly rich diversity of habitats, ranging from seashore, reedbed and lagoon to heathland and mixed and pine woodland. From the 16th century onwards, successive owners of Brownsea have enriched the island with extensive tree planting. Red squirrels, safe from their mainland predators, the grey squirrel, still survive in the pinewoods. Colourful peacocks abound and shy Sika deer, introduced in Victorian times, can occasionally be seen. At least 60 types of tree now grow on Brownsea, and they support a wide variety of birdlife, including treecreeper, woodpecker, jay, woodcock and tawny owl. The island also supports many important populations of dragonfly, butterfly and lizard. The northern part of the island, leased by the Dorset Wildlife Trust, contains several fresh water lakes and a lagoon. The latter was formed when land, reclaimed in the 1850s, was allowed to be flooded again in the 1930s. Its brick sea wall now encloses 100 acres of non-tidal sea water, marshland and reedbed that attract many species of wading birds. Summer visitors, such as tern and passing migrants, are also regular visitors to the lagoon.

ROBERT BADEN-POWELL

The hero of the siege of Mafeking during the Boer War, Robert Baden-Powell, was invited by the then owner of Brownsea Island, Charles van Raalte, to hold his first Scout camp there. The success of this venture in August 1907 led Baden-Powell to form the Scouting movement. Today the camp is used by Scouts and Guides from around the world. A carved stone monument on the island commemorates this historic event.

ISLAND WALKS

A network of tracks and paths criss-cross this 500 acre island. For details on access to the nature reserve contact the Dorset Wildlife Trust (tel. 01202 709445). There is no public access to Brownsea Castle or its grounds.

PLACES TO VISIT

- Brownsea Open Air Theatre
- Dorset Wildlife Trust Reserve
- Site of Baden-Powell's first Scout camp
- Mid-19th century St Mary's church
- Site of 19th century pottery

Above *This kiln is all that remains of an ill-fated plan to develop Brownsea in the 1850s as a centre for making fine china. The scheme failed, as the clay was too coarse and suitable only for making drainage pipes and bricks.*

Below *The beach on the southwest coast of the island is littered with reminders of its former pottery industry.*

ISLE OF WIGHT

Once the home of dinosaurs and inhabited by man for at least 10,000 years, England's largest island has played an important role in the shaping of our country's history. From Roman occupation to the threat of Nazi invasion, the Isle of Wight's inhabitants have suffered many periods of war and peace. Patronised by artists, writers, poets and royalty during the 19th century, the island not only became a popular destination for visitors but was also in the forefront of technological innovation. Today, with its equable climate, miles of clean, sandy beaches, natural beauty and rich historical legacy, the Isle of Wight has become the destination for nearly three million visitors a year.

Above *Owned by the National Trust, the well preserved Elizabethan manor house at Mottistone is tucked away in a sleepy village below Westover Down. Only the gardens are open to the public.*

Right *An Area of Outstanding Natural Beauty, Tennyson Down is the highest point on the island's coastline. Its chalk downland is dominated by the monument erected in memory of the poet Alfred, Lord Tennyson, who lived in nearby Freshwater from 1853 until his death in 1892.*

HISTORY

Evidence in the form of flint tools has been found to show that the Isle of Wight has been inhabited by man for at least 10,000 years. However, it did not become the island as we know it until around 6000BC, when The Solent was formed by rising sea levels. Around 3000BC, people from the New Stone Age were farming on the island and a long barrow, or grave, from this period can be seen today just north of Mottistone. Many artefacts from the Beaker culture of the Bronze Age, around 1500BC, have also been discovered on the island.

The Romans arrived on the Isle of Wight, or Vectis as they called it, around 50AD. For the next 400 years, they lived in peaceful co-existence with the locals and set up farms and vineyards around their smart villas. Well preserved remains of two Roman villas, with mosaic floors, bath houses and central heating, can be seen today at Newport and Brading.

The Romans withdrew from Britain around 410AD, and the Isle of Wight soon became a target for pagan Saxon invaders. After much bloodshed, peace was restored when the Christian West Saxon king, Caedwalla, conquered the island in 686AD and converted it to

Christianity. There then followed 200 years of stability until the late 9th century, when the Danes swept in from the north and brought death and destruction to the populace. Peace only returned to the island following the Norman invasion of England in 1066.

Under the Normans, the lordship of the Isle of Wight was granted to William Fitz-Osbern, steward to William the Conqueror. Carisbrooke Castle, near Newport, was built by Fitz-Osbern on the site of a Saxon fortification. Around 1100, the lordship passed to Richard de Redvers and it remained in his family until the end of the 13th century, when fears of a French invasion led the Crown to take control of the island. These fears

were soon realised, and for nearly 250 years the Isle of Wight was in the front line in wars against France. During the reign of Henry VIII, major defensive fortifications were built at Cowes, Sandown and Yarmouth, and the well-preserved Tudor remains of the latter castle can still be seeen today. Many islanders were killed by French raiding parties, but a temporary peace settled on the island when French landings were finally repulsed by Richard Worsley, Governor of the Isle of Wight, in 1545.

This peace only lasted for 40 years before the Isle of Wight was once again threatened by invasion, this time by the Spanish. Despite the defeat of the Armada in 1588, the threat of Spanish

Above *The chalk ridge that runs across the centre of the Isle of Wight ends dramatically at The Needles. Perched on the westerly of these famous sea stacks is the lighthouse, automated since 1994, which began operating in 1859. A historic site, the crumbling headland is the site of a Victorian battery and, in more recent times, the test firing of the British Black Knight rocket engines.*

invasion remained for some years and, to counter this threat, Carisbrooke Castle was enlarged.

The English Civil War started in 1642 and the Isle of Wight easily fell to Parliamentary forces under Cromwell. In 1647, Charles I was imprisoned in Carisbrooke Castle until he was returned

to London for his trial and execution. Following the restoration of the monarchy in 1661, the island entered another period of peace and by the 18th century, improved farming methods such as wool production, and industry such as boatbuilding, both helped to boost employment. By the 19th century, the Isle of Wight had also become a popular destination, not only for artists, writers and poets such as Turner, Keats and Tennyson, but also for wealthy middle class visitors and royalty. In 1844, Queen Victoria purchased Osborne House as a summer retreat, and this royal patronage further boosted the island's image as a fashionable resort. Regular steamship sailings to and from the mainland, the expansion of coastal towns such as Ventnor, Shanklin, Ryde and Cowes and the building of a network of railways all contributed to its success and prosperity.

However, during this period of growth, the island was once again under the threat of invasion from France. Due to the Isle of Wight's strategic position overlooking the approaches to The Solent, Spithead and the naval base at Portsmouth, a series of coastal and sea forts were built between 1860 and 1880 at the western and eastern ends of the island. A new military road was also built along the southwest coast, but the threatened invasion never came. Many of the forts, with modifications, continued in use well into the 20th century. The Needles Battery became one of the

earliest radar stations during World War II and, from 1956 to 1971, was the test site for the Saunders-Roe Black Knight and Black Arrow rocket engines.

During World War II, the Isle of Wight was, yet again, in the front line of the defence of Britain. With the real threat of a German invasion, the island was heavily fortified and became a restricted zone.

Below *The south coast is dominated by both chalk and fossil-rich sedimentary rocks. Here, the chalk cliffs sweep around the clear blue waters of Compton Bay to secluded Freshwater Bay and, beyond, the majestic 482ft-high Tennyson Down.*

Warship and aircraft construction at Cowes and a string of the world's first radar stations sited on the Downs all became targets for the Luftwaffe. During the build-up to D-Day in 1944, ships carrying 130,000 Allied troops assembled off the southeast coast of the island before making their journey to the Normandy beach heads. Fuel for the Allied invasion of Europe was pumped from Shanklin through a 70-mile long pipeline, known as PLUTO, under the English Channel to Cherbourg in northern France.

The 20th century also saw continued growth not only in tourism, but also in industry, on the island. Companies such as J. Samuel White and S. E. Saunders were in the forefront of seaplane development during the First World War. Based at East Cowes, Saunder-Roe, as it became known in 1929, went on to produce the giant *Princess* flying boat of the early 1950s, the world's first practical hovercraft in 1959, helicopters, rocket-jet aircraft and rocket engines. The Isle of Wight's aviation tradition has been continued into the 21st century by Britten-Norman who produce their short take-off and landing Islander aircraft at Bembridge.

Both industry and tourism continue to prosper on the Isle of Wight in the 21st century. Major international events such as the Isle of Wight Festival (held in early June) and Cowes Week (held at the end of July/early August) attract hundreds of thousands of visitors from around the world. More importantly the island, with its above-average summer sunshine, clean, sandy beaches, picturesque villages, rolling downs, wooded valleys and rich historical legacy continues to attract traditional family holidaymakers.

NATURAL HISTORY

The Isle of Wight is a geologist's paradise. During the Cretaceous period, over 100 million years ago, this part of the world had a sub-tropical climate and was home to herds of roaming dinosaurs. The crumbling sedimentary rocks along the southwest coast of the island, notably in the cliffs around Brightstone and Brook Bays, are some of the most important locations for dinosaur fossils in Europe.

A chalk ridge runs along the centre of the island and is seen in its dramatic conclusion in the cliffs around Compton Bay, Tennyson Down and at The Needles. To the north are the sands and clays of the low-lying coastal plain.

The diversity of the island's geology has, in turn, provided a rich variety of wildlife habitats. The chalk downland, largely untouched by farming, is home to a large number of species of wildflower, butterfly, insect and nesting birds.

From the flat tidal creeks of the north coast to the rocky seashores and cliffs of the south coast, the island's 60 mile coastline also offers a wide variety of habitats. Inland, woodlands are important sites for wildflowers, the dormouse, red squirrel and rare butterflies such as the brimstone.

About half of the Isle of Wight's 147 square miles are now classified as Areas of Outstanding Natural Beauty, of which one of the most famous is Tennyson Down. The island also has 40 Sites of Special Scientific Interest (SSSI), many of

which are internationally recognised for their importance. Of these, the Newtown Harbour Nature Reserve, managed by the National Trust, is one of the most outstanding. On the northern coast of the island, the reserve contains extensive untouched areas of saltmarsh, mudflats, ancient meadow and woodland. These habitats support a number of rare species from red squirrel to white admiral butterfly and orchid. The adjoining estuary is an important wintering ground for large numbers of visiting wildfowl and waders.

Other important internationally recognised sites on the island include: Arreton Down, Rew Down, Dodnor Creek and Nansen Hill. Near the east coast, the lagoons, reedbeds and meadows of Brading Marshes which support a wide variety of insect, plant and birdlife have recently become the first RSPB reserve on the island.

HOW TO GET THERE

By sea Wightlink operate the following services to the Isle of Wight: Portsmouth to Ryde (Fast Cat passenger);

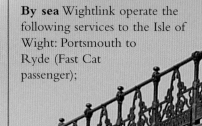

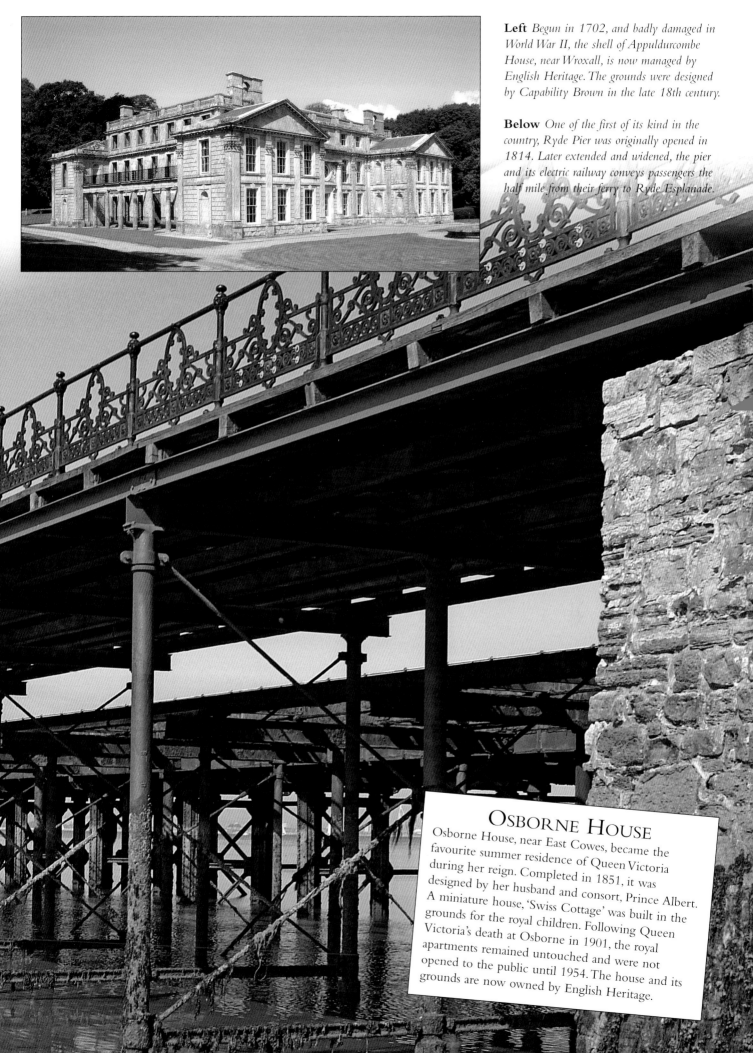

Left *Begun in 1702, and badly damaged in World War II, the shell of Appuldurcombe House, near Wroxall, is now managed by English Heritage. The grounds were designed by Capability Brown in the late 18th century.*

Below *One of the first of its kind in the country, Ryde Pier was originally opened in 1814. Later extended and widened, the pier and its electric railway conveys passengers the half mile from their ferry to Ryde Esplanade.*

OSBORNE HOUSE

Osborne House, near East Cowes, became the favourite summer residence of Queen Victoria during her reign. Completed in 1851, it was designed by her husband and consort, Prince Albert. A miniature house, 'Swiss Cottage' was built in the grounds for the royal children. Following Queen Victoria's death at Osborne in 1901, the royal apartments remained untouched and were not opened to the public until 1954. The house and its grounds are now owned by English Heritage.

Left *The Isle of Wight Steam Railway, based at Haven Street, takes its passengers back in time along five miles of preserved railway between Smallbrook Junction and Wootton.*

813818 or visit the Isle of Wight Tourist Information website: www.isleofwight.com

WHERE TO STAY

The Isle of Wight offers a huge choice of accommodation from caravan and camping sites to self-catering units, guesthouses and hotels. For further details of accommodation contact the Tourist Information Centre (tel. 01983 813813). Website: www.isleofwight.com

ISLAND WALKS

With its long, dramatic coastline, beaches, rolling downland and woodland, and over 500 miles of rights of way, the Isle of Wight offers an enormous choice of walking. The 68-mile Isle of Wight Coastal Footpath is a designated long distance path around the perimeter of the island. There are also seven major long distance trails:
1. The Tennyson Trail is a 13 mile path from Alum Bay to Carisbrooke
2. The Hamstead Trail is an 8 mile path from Freshwater to Newtown
3. The Shepherds Trail is a 10 mile path from Carisbrooke to Atherfield
4. The Worsley Trail is a 15 mile path from Shanklin to Brightstone Forest

Portsmouth to Fishbourne (car and passenger ferry); Lymington to Yarmouth (car and passenger ferry). For details contact Wightlink (tel. 0870 582 7744) or visit their website: www.wightlink.co.uk

Red Funnel also operate the following services to the island: Southampton to West Cowes (Red Jet hi-speed passengers only); Southampton to East Cowes (car and passenger ferry). For details contact Red Funnel (tel. 0870 444 8898) or visit their website: www.redfunnel.co.uk

A fast hovercraft service for passengers operates between Southsea and Ryde. For details contact Hovertravel (tel. 01983 811000) or visit their website: www.hovertravel.co.uk

ORDNANCE SURVEY MAPS

Landranger 1:50,000 series No. 196

TOURIST INFORMATION

There are Tourist Information Centres in Cowes, Newport, Ryde, Sandown, Shanklin, Ventnor and Yarmouth. For general information telephone 01983

5. The Stenbury Trail is a 12 mile path from Shide, near Newport, to Ventnor
6. The Bembridge Trail is a 15 mile path from Slide, near Newport, to Bembridge
7. The Nunwell Trail is a 10 mile path from Ryde to Sandown

PLACES TO VISIT
● The Needles Battery (National Trust)
● Tennyson Down and Monument

● Alum Bay
● Quarr Abbey
● Isle of Wight Steam Railway
● Appuldurcombe House (English Heritage)
● Osborne House (English Heritage)
● Arreton Manor
● Carisbrooke Castle (English Heritage)
● Nunwell House
● Brading Roman villa
● Newtown Nature Reserve (National Trust)
● Brading Marshes Reserve (RSPB)
● Mottistone Manor (National Trust)

Above *This Noah's Ark lookalike, other eccentric, converted houseboats and a unique 'flotel' all rub shoulders along the shores of Bembridge Harbour.*

Below *Attracted by its miles of sandy beaches, beautiful scenery, historic sites and above-average sunshine, nearly three million visitors a year now come to the Isle of Wight. Here, at Sandown on the east coast, summer holidaymakers enjoy the clean sandy beach and safe bathing. The 68-mile Isle of Wight Coastal Path passes along the clifftops and around distant Culver Cliff.*

HAYLING ISLAND

Populated since the Stone Age, low-lying Hayling Island was for centuries a remote home for farmers and fishermen. Suffering from flooding and plague in the 14th century, the island slumbered on into the early 20th century. During the 19th century, grandiose plans to turn it into a resort failed to attract visitors, although the arrival of the railway in 1867 certainly improved communications with the mainland. It was not until the 1930s that Hayling was developed into the popular resort that it is today.

HISTORY

Excavations have discovered that low-lying Hayling Island has probably been occupied since Stone Age times. Bronze Age man was followed by the Romans, who built a temple on the island. Following the departure of the Romans, Anglo-Saxons built several hamlets on the island, supported by farming and fishing. Following the Norman Conquest in 1066, the majority of Hayling Island, South Hayling Manor, was granted to the French Benedictine Abbey of Jemièges, a situation which existed until 1415. By the time of the Domesday Book, the production of salt from seawater had become an important local industry, while oyster farming later developed into a further source of income.

During the first half of the 14th century, hundreds of acres of farmland were permanently lost to the sea in a great flood, and it is estimated that half of the island's population died during the Black Death.

In 1579, South Hayling Manor became the property of the Dukes of Norfolk who owned it until 1825, when it was sold to William Padwick. A toll bridge from the mainland had opened the previous year, but grandiose plans to develop Hayling into a fashionable resort came to nothing. Links with the mainland improved in 1865, when the railway line from Havant was opened for goods trains as far as Langstone.

Above *In an attempt to develop Hayling Island as a resort, the grand Crescent and neighbouring Royal Hotel were built in 1825. Due to lack of public support, nothing came of these grandiose plans and it was only in the 1930s that Hayling became a popular seaside resort.*

The route to South Hayling was completed in 1867 and passenger services started in July of that year. This coincided with the opening of a racecourse and grandstand in front of the Royal Hotel. However, public patronage was poor and Hayling continued to slumber on until the early 20th century.

Below *Hayling Island has over three miles of European Blue Flag shingle beaches along the seafront facing The Solent. Windsurfing, invented on the island, and sailing are two of the many water sports that are enjoyed around the coastline.*

Above *Hayling Island's Funland Amusement Park is located next to the beach. The East Hayling Light Railway terminates here after meandering its way through the sand dunes from East Hayling.*

Hayling Island's development as a resort started in earnest in the 1930s. New houses, cinemas, a funfair and holiday camps were built, and thousands of visitors descended on the island during the summer months.

World War II soon brought an end to this, and Hayling's proximity to Portsmouth and its important naval base put the island in the front line. To draw German bombers away from their main target, fires were lit around the coast of Hayling and on the small islands in Langstone Harbour during air raids to simulate bomb damage. Although the ploy was successful, Hayling suffered more than its fair share of damage. Two anti-aircraft batteries were set up on the island and remains of these can still be seen at Sinah Common. During 1943, in preparation for the invasion of Europe and under a cloak of utmost secrecy, concrete artificial harbours, known as Mulberry Harbours, were built around Hayling's coastline. Remains of one of these enormous concrete caissons and the construction site can still be seen today.

After the war, Hayling's development continued apace, with more new houses, schools, churches and a library being built. Since 1950, the island's population has increased threefold to its present day total of over 16,000. The old wooden

Below *Much sought after beach huts line the extensive shingle beach that overlooks Hayling Bay and The Solent.*

road bridge over Langstone Harbour was replaced by a modern concrete structure in 1956. Sadly, the cost of renewing the old timber railway bridge was prohibitive and the line from Havant was closed on 2 November 1963. The stumps of the bridge can still be seen today in Langstone Harbour. Since closure, the former trackbed has become the Hayling Billy Trail for walkers, cyclists and horse riders. The former goods shed at South Hayling is now used as a theatre.

NATURAL HISTORY
Rich in fish, the shallow waters around Hayling attract many species of seabird. Langstone Harbour is a favourite haunt of grebe, in particular the great crested, black-necked and Slavonian varieties. Winter visitors range from diving duck, such as the red-breasted merganser, to great northern diver, razorbill, guillemot and cormorant.

During the spring, migratrory seabirds, such as tern, skua, gannet and fulmar pass through Hayling on their journey to northern breeding grounds. In the summer, sandwich, common and little tern arrive to breed on the small RSPB-protected islands at the northern end of Langstone Harbour. Common seal are also increasingly seen in the waters of Chichester Harbour.

Old oysterbeds at the north of Hayling have been made into artificial islands which are now successful breeding grounds for oystercatcher, ringed plover and little tern.

A breeding ground for whitethroat and linnet and home to rare plantlife, the area of heathland, grassland and sand dunes at Sandy Point at the eastern end of the island is now a nature reserve owned by Hampshire County Council.

HOW TO GET THERE
By road take the A3023 from Havant across Langstone Bridge. A ferry for foot passengers also operates between Ferry Point at the west end of the island and Eastney Bridge, Portsmouth.

ORDNANCE SURVEY MAPS
Landranger 1:50,000 series No. 197

TOURIST INFORMATION
Hayling Island Tourist Information Centre, Central Beachlands, Seafront, Hayling Island PO11 OAG (tel. 023 9246 7111). Website: www.havant.gov.uk

WHERE TO STAY
Hayling Island offers a wide variety of accommodation, from a caravan and camping site to self-catering units, guesthouses and hotels. For further details contact the Tourist Information Centre (see above).

ISLAND WALKS
In addition to the many footpaths on the island the Hayling Billy Trail, also suitable for cyclists and horse riders, follows the route of the old railway line from the Station Theatre to Langstone Bridge.

PLACES TO VISIT

- Station Theatre
- Hayling Billy Trail
- Funfair
- East Hayling Light Railway
- Sandy Point Nature Reserve
- World War II gunning placements and remains of Mulberry Harbours at Sinah Common and adjacent beach

- Norfolk Crescent
- 13th century St Mary's Church, South Hayling
- 13th century St Peter's Church, North Hayling. In the churchyard is the grave of Princess Yourievsky, illegitimate daughter of Czar Alexander II of Russia, who lived on Hayling Island from 1932 until her death in 1959.

Above *A lone signal watches over the remains of the old railway bridge across Langstone Harbour. To the right is the modern concrete road bridge which opened in 1956, replacing the previous timber structure. Due to the cost of replacing the old railway bridge, the branch line from Havant to Hayling Island closed in November 1963. The trackbed now forms the route of the Hayling Billy Trail.*

THORNEY ISLAND

Thorney Island, or the 'Island of Thorns' was, until the 1930s, the home of poor farmers and fishermen who eked out a living in a flat landscape set amidst the marshlands and mudflats of Chichester Harbour. All this changed in the 1930s when, with the clouds of war in Europe gathering, the RAF took over the island and constructed a large airfield. Today, the island is still owned by the Ministry of Defence, but visitors can continue to enjoy the tranquil beauty of the area and its abundant birdlife by walking along a dedicated coastal footpath.

Above *Built by Bishop Warlewaste in the 12th century, St Nicholas Church is located close to the coastal path around Thorney Island. Permission is required from the MOD to visit the church.*

HISTORY
Located in the marshlands of Chichester Harbour, Thorney was for centuries a remote farming and fishing settlement. In 1086, the survey for Domesday Book found that the island was held by Bishop Osbern, who let it to a man named Mauger. For centuries the farmers and fishermen living in the small village of West Thorney scratched a living from the land and sea. Although rising sea levels encroached upon their land, it was not until the 19th century that substantial sea defences were built. In 1870, marshland to the north of the island was reclaimed, leaving only the Great Deep and Little Deep separating it from the mainland. Thorney was taken over by the RAF in 1935 and the large airfield was officially opened in 1938. During World War II, it was an important base for Coastal Command aircraft and played a major role in support of the D-Day landings in 1944. The airfield finally closed in 1976 and, in 1980, became a temporary home for Vietnamese refugees. The former airfield was finally taken over by the Army in 1982 and renamed Baker Barracks. It is currently occupied by the 47th Field Regiment, Royal Artillery.

NATURAL HISTORY
Thorney Island is located in Chichester Harbour, an Area of Outstanding Natural Beauty, and internationally famous for its estuarine birds. The coastal footpath around the island is a favourite spot for birdwatchers, especially during winter months when the native waders are joined by visiting wildfowl. Ducks, geese and waders abound, the former found in the old saltmarsh channels and the latter feeding at low tide on the extensive mud flats. In summer, reed and sedge-warbler

are abundant in the reedbeds. The summer months are also the best time to see the wide variety of plants – including glasswort, sea lavender and sea beet – that grow in the saltmarshes and the golden samphire that grows along the sea wall.

HOW TO GET THERE
On foot from the village of Emsworth. Parking available in the village.

ORDNANCE SURVEY MAPS
Landranger 1:50,000 series No. 197

TOURIST INFORMATION
Nearest office: Havant Tourist Information Centre, 1 Park Road South, Havant, Hampshire PO9 1HA (tel. 023 9248 0024). Website: www.havant.gov.uk

WHERE TO STAY
Accommodation available in Emsworth and surrounding area. Contact Havant Tourist Information Centre (see above).

ISLAND WALK
The only public access to Thorney Island is along a seven-mile footpath that follows the shoreline and offers glorious views of Chichester Harbour. As Thorney Island is owned by the Ministry of Defence visitors must enter and exit through steel gates at each end of the footpath. These gates are connected by an intercom to the security guard at the main gatehouse. Names and addresses are requested and once through the gate walkers must strictly adhere to the marked footpath. For details of this fascinating walk visit www.walkingbritain.co.uk and go to Walk a043.

Care should also be exercised during times of high spring tides. For further details on tide times visit the Chichester Harbour Conservancy website: www.conservancy.co.uk

Above *The coastal path around Thorney Island offers wonderful views over Chichester Harbour. The MOD land that it encloses is strictly out of bounds!*

Below *The old landing lights for the former RAF airfield on Thorney Island stand like lonely sentinels in the mud flats of Chichester Harbour. During World War II it was an important base for RAF Coastal Command and home to famous aircraft such as Beauforts, Blenheims, Liberators and Hudsons.*

ISLE OF SHEPPEY

Over the centuries, the Isle of Sheppey has seen its fair share of foreign invaders. Following occupation by the Romans and their withdrawal in the early 5th century, the island was invaded by the Saxons before becoming part of the Anglo-Saxon kingdom of Kent. During the 9th century, Viking raiders attacked the island before they, in turn, settled there. Peace returned under the Normans and, by the 14th century, the Isle of Sheppey had become strategically important, not only for the defence of the important Medway Estuary but also as a major exporter of Kent wool. Briefly seized by the Dutch in 1667, the town of Sheerness became an important royal dockyard and is still a thriving freight-handling port. Plans to develop the island's east coast as a major holiday resort in the early 20th century failed to materialise and, today, the island's charm lies mainly in the wildlife and marshlands of its south coast.

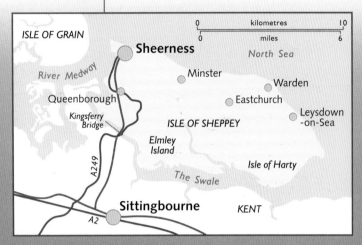

Below *Home to wading birds and birds of prey, Harty Marshes extends for several miles along the southeast coast of the Isle of Sheppey. Here, overlooking the stretch of water known as The Swale and close to the remote Ferry Inn, is all that remains of a once-important ferry crossing to the Kent mainland near Faversham.*

HISTORY

The Isle of Sheppey has been inhabited by man for at least 6,000 years. Following a period of occupation by the Romans, the island was invaded and finally settled by the Saxons, and Sheppey became part of the Anglo-Saxon kingdom of Kent. During the early 7th century, the Anglo-Saxon king of Kent, Aethelberht, was converted to Christianity and, in 675AD, a monastery for nuns was founded at Minster by Queen Seaxburga. By the end of the 8th century, however, the Isle of Sheppey and surrounding areas had become the target for attack by the Vikings. Following half a century of

SS RICHARD MONTGOMERY

In August 1944, an American Liberty ship, the *SS Richard Montgomery*, arrived in the Thames Estuary carrying over 6,000 tons of munitions for the Allied war effort in Europe. While waiting to join a convoy, the ship ran aground on treacherous sand banks just over a mile out to sea from the port of Sheerness. Around half of the explosives were successfully salvaged before the wreck was deemed unsafe and abandoned. A continuing hazard to shipping, the position of the wreck and its deadly and unstable cargo is well marked by buoys. However, over 60 years later, the population of Sheerness still live with the threat of a massive explosion and the ensuing tidal wave!

raids, the Vikings settled on Sheppey, destroying the monastery and building forts. Peace only settled on the island after the Norman invasion in 1066.

Due to its position close to the estuaries of the Medway and Thames rivers, the Isle of Sheppey had always been strategically important for shipping. The stretch of water separating the island from the mainland, known as The Swale, was also a vitally important route for ships sailing between the Thames and the Medway to the English Channel. To protect this route, a castle was built at Queenborough in the 1360s by Edward III. A town and harbour grew up around the castle and, in 1368, it became a royal borough and one of only two ports in Kent which were allowed to export wool. Queenborough was briefly occupied by the Dutch in 1667 when they attacked and destroyed British navy ships in the Medway and Thames estuaries.

In 1665, during the reign of Charles II, Sheerness was chosen by Samuel Pepys – the Chief Secretary to the Admiralty – as the site for a new royal dockyard. In 1667, before it was completed, Sheerness bore the brunt of an attack by the Dutch Navy. For a short time they occupied the fort and town while their warships

Above *Originally the site of a ferry, the first combined road and rail bridge across The Swale to to the Isle of Sheppey was opened in 1860. The present Kingsferry Bridge, with an electrically operated lifting section to allow the passage of ships, was built in 1959. Behind it is the new Sheppey Crossing bridge that was opened for road traffic in July 2006. During its construction, archæologists discovered artefacts dating from the Iron Age and the Roman occupation.*

KING JAMES II

The last Roman Catholic monarch of England, Scotland and Ireland, James II of England was deeply unpopular with his subjects and, especially, the Anglican Church. Ignominiously unseated from his throne by William of Orange, James attempted to flee to the safety of France in December 1688. Crossing The Swale to the Isle of Sheppey, James was captured in the Elmley Marshes and taken to Faversham in Kent. However, he later escaped from custody to complete his journey to France.

destroyed 15 Royal Navy ships moored in the Medway. Sheerness remained a royal dockyard until 1962, when it was closed.

For hundreds of years until the 19th century, the Isle of Sheppey's links with the mainland had been provided by two ferries across The Swale. One, at the narrowest part of The Swale, was at King's Ferry. The other was between the Isle of Harty in the southeast of the island to a point on the mainland two miles north of Faversham. King's Ferry

was replaced by a railway and road bridge in 1860 and the Harty Ferry ceased to operate in the early 20th century.

The coming of the London Chatham & Dover Railway to Sheerness in 1860 greatly enhanced the town's importance as a port. Rail-connected ferry services were also operated from Queenborough to Flushing in Holland. Now the Isle of Sheppey's largest town, Sheerness is not only an important freight-handling port but also home to a large steel works.

At the beginning of the 20th century, Sheppey was an important focal point for early aviation development. A small airfield and flying club was established at Eastchurch and famous aviation pioneers such as Charles Rolls and the Short Brothers were regular visitors.

Also in the early 20th century, attempts were made to develop the eastern coast of Sheppey as a seaside resort. A light railway was opened in 1901 from the main railway line at Queenborough to the new resort of

Leysdown-on-Sea. The attempts to poularise Leysdown as a resort for Londoners was never a complete success and the railway closed in 1950. Today, the resort is more well known for its many self-catering caravan parks and amusement arcades.

Located to the south of Eastchurch, in the centre of the island, is a different aspect of the Isle of Sheppey: on the site of the early aviation pioneers' airfield are now three of Her Majesty's Prisons, housing over 2,000 inmates.

NATURAL HISTORY

Much of the Isle of Sheppey is low-lying, and the southern half of the island contains one of the largest areas of wetland in the UK. Some parts of this have been reclaimed as farmland, but the majority is still a haven for wildlife. In the southwest of the island, Elmley Marshes - now an RSPB Nature Reserve - attracts many wading birds, ducks and geese. During the winter, it is also a popular location for seeing birds of prey. To the southeast is the Swale National Nature Reserve, which is also a Site of Special Scientific Interest and a Special Protection Area. Located in the Harty

Marshes, the reserve extends for several miles along the coast from Shell Ness to the Ferry Inn public house. Not only an important site for wading birds and birds of prey, the nature reserve also supports many rare plants, butterflies and moths.

HOW TO GET THERE

By road The A249 (Junction 5 of the M2) crosses the River Swale on the new Sheppey Bridge.

By rail Stations on the Isle of Sheppey at Queenborough and Sheerness are served by local trains from Sittingbourne.

ORDNANCE SURVEY MAPS

Landranger 1:50,000 series No. 178

TOURIST INFORMATION

The nearest Tourist Information Centre is at Faversham in Kent:
Faversham Tourist Information Centre, Fleur de Lis Heritage Centre, 13 Preston Street, Faversham,

Below *The shingle beach at Leysdown-on-Sea is a popular spot for fishing. A designated EU bathing beach, at low tide Leysdown has one of the few sandy beaches on the island. To the south is an official naturist beach.*

Kent ME13 8NS (tel. 01795 534542) or visit their website: www.faversham.org

WHERE TO STAY

There are very few hotels and other establishments offering accommodation on the Isle of Sheppey. For details contact the Faversham Tourist Information Centre (see above). However, there are a total of six caravan and camping sites on the island.

ISLAND WALKS

There are footpaths in the area of Harty Marshes in the southeast of the island and also to the RSPB reserve at Elmley Marshes in the southwest of the island.

PLACES TO VISIT

- The Ferry Inn, Isle of Harty
- Queenborough Museum
- RSPB reserve at Elmley Marshes
- Swale National Nature Reserve
- Remains of Minster Abbey

Right *Built in 1902, this ornately decorated clocktower dominates the pedestrianised town centre of Sheerness. The nearby church of St Henry and Elizabeth was designed by E W Pugin in 1863.*

Below *A popular destination for families during the summer months, the island of Mersea has, since Roman times, been a favourite haunt for those seeking rest and recreation. A curious mixture of either total remoteness or seething masses, the low-lying estuarine islands of Eastern England are among the least well-known of those around our coastline and are well worth visiting.*

EASTERN ENGLAND

CANVEY ISLAND
FOULNESS ISLAND
WALLASEA ISLAND
NORTHEY ISLAND
MERSEA ISLAND

CANVEY ISLAND

From Roman times until the end of the 19th century, low-lying Canvey Island was a windswept stretch of frequently flooded marshland and sheep pasture inhabited by a few hardy souls. Early 20th century plans to develop Canvey into a holiday resort for Londoners ran into financial problems, but the inter-war years saw a rapid growth in house building and visitor numbers. Following the disastrous floods of 1953, house building continued apace and today, much of the eastern half of the island is taken over by homes for over 45,000 people.

HISTORY

Artefacts unearthed on Canvey Island show that it has been inhabited by man since the late Stone Age. Other artefacts dating from the Bronze and Iron Ages show a continuation of human settlement. The Romans also occupied Canvey, and it is likely that they used it as a port of call on their way to London. It was probably around this time that Canvey became separated from the mainland, due to rising sea levels and land subsidence. Salt manufacturing, and sheep farming on the island's fertile soil, were the two principle activities of islanders during the Roman occupation. Over many centuries, the sale of sheep's cheese (and later cow's cheese) to passing ships and the London markets was the main source of income for Canvey's islanders.

Following the Roman withdrawal

during the early 5th century, Canvey Island was settled by the Saxons and became part of the Kingdom of Essex. From the 7th century the Saxons were converted to Christianity, but there is no evidence to suggest they built a church on Canvey at this time. During the 9th century, the whole of this region was subject to attack by Viking raiders from Denmark. Having set up bases around

Left *Originally built as part of World War II coastal defences, the Art Deco style Labworth Cafe on Canvey's seafront was designed by the leading Anglo-Danish architect Sir Ove Arup in the 1940s. Refurbished in 1998, this historic building offers visitors a grandstand view of the Thames Estuary.*

Shoebury and Benfleet, they planned to sail up the River Thames and attack London, but were defeated by King Alfred's forces at the Battle of Benfleet in 896AD. Later, during the reign of Henry II in the 12th century, Canvey Island's land was divided up between nine parishes, a situation which manifested itself as a major problem in later years!

Always a major problem in the Thames estuary, land subsidence and rising sea levels were already causing severe flooding on Canvey Island by the Middle Ages. By the 14th century, attempts had been made to build rudimentary sea defences, but it was not until the 17th century that a major plan was put forward to enclose the whole island with a seawall. In 1622, Dutch engineers and workmen, already experienced in building sea defences and drainage systems in Lincolnshire, were contracted to carry out the work. After

Above *The Monico pub near Canvey's seafront was once an important meeting place for local musicians in the early 1970s. Nearby is Astaire's nightclub where locally-based band, Dr Feelgood, first performed on stage in 1971.*

successfully enclosing a large part of the island, many of the Dutch workers received parcels of land in lieu of payment. Some built distinctive small octagonal cottages on their land and settled there with their families, forming a close-knit Dutch community on the island. One of these cottages has been preserved and is now the Dutch Cottage Museum. Most of the Dutch settlers left Canvey Island during a series of Anglo-Dutch wars between 1652 and 1674. In 1667, the Dutch fleet made a successful foray up the Thames towards London, raiding Canvey Island in the process.

With the Dutch gone from the island, the sea defences soon fell into disrepair and serious flooding occurred on many occasions. Disputes about ownership of land and

DR FEELGOOD

The pub-rock band *Dr Feelgood*, named after a Johnny Kidd & the Pirates song of the same name, was formed in 1971 by members who had all played in bars around Canvey Island and Southend-on-Sea. Their debut album *Down by the Jetty* was released by United Artists in 1974. *Stupidity*, a live album released in 1976, reached No.1 in the UK album charts. Sadly, the band's inspirational lead singer Lee Brilleaux died of cancer in 1994 soon after recording the band's final album, *Down at the Doctor's*.

TWO TREE ISLAND

Two Tree Island lies only a short distance northeast of Canvey Island and is easily accessible from Leigh-on-Sea railway station. This small island was formed during land reclamation in the 18th century and later used as a site for a sewage works and for landfill. The island is split into two by a road that ends in a car park and a slipway. The western half is part of the Hadleigh Castle Country Park estate and is used for recreational activities, while the eastern half is known as Leigh National Nature Reserve and is managed by the Essex Wildlife Trust. It is an internationally important site for overwintering Brent goose and also designated a Site of Special Scientific Interest due to the rare plantlife that has grown up around the old sewage works.

where responsibility lay for repairing the sea walls dragged on for years until it was resolved by an Act of Parliament in 1792. The turning point for Canvey Island came in 1897, when strong winds and high tides coincided to severely breach the seawall and flood large areas of farmland. This, together with a nationwide slump in the agricultural industry, led many landowners on the island to sell up and move away.

Taking advantage of this situation, London entrepreneur Frederick Hester snapped up much of the land, built bungalows for Londoners wishing to escape the grime of the capital, and

started to develop the island as a holiday resort. By 1905, however, his grandiose schemes - including a glass Winter Garden pavilion, Venetian canal and an electric railway - ground to a halt and Hester became bankrupt.

After World War I, Canvey became a popular destination for thousands of day trippers from London. House building continued and the population steadily increased from 300 in 1901 to 3,000 in 1924. This increase in numbers of both visitors and residents put severe strain on the one ferry service across Benfleet Creek to the mainland. Plans for a bridge had been put forward as early as 1900,

but it was not until the early 1930s that it was built. This physical connection with the mainland brought an enormous upsurge in development on Canvey Island and, by 1938, the population had risen to 6,500. By the beginning of World War II new housing estates, shops, schools and even a casino had been built in the eastern half of the island, while a large oil storage depot and jetties were opened at the western end.

During World War II, Canvey's stategically important oil storage facilities and its proximity to London made it a prime target for attack by German bombers. Coastal defences and anti-

aircraft sites were installed to counter attacks from the air and sea but, by the end of the war, over 50 local people had been killed.

After the war, house building continued apace on Canvey and, by 1953, the population had risen to 11,000. However, tragedy struck the island early in the morning of 1 February 1953, when strong winds and high tides created an enormous surge of water that breached the supposedly impregnable sea defences. Although severe flooding occurred all along the east coast of Britain, Canvey Island probably suffered the most. In all, 58 people lost their lives and over 10,000 were made homeless.

Since the 1953 disaster, Canvey's sea defences have been greatly strengthened and an early warning system has been installed. Although there has been little further industrial development, house building has continued at a great pace and the population currently stands at over 45,000. However, Canvey's appeal as as a tourist destination has certainly not kept up with the island's development into a massive housing estate. Along the seafront, sheltered from the tides by the massive concrete seawalls, are tacky amusement arcades, nightclubs, pubs and funfairs that all seem to belong to a past era when tens of thousands of east Londoners would descend on the island on a single Bank Holiday!

NATURAL HISTORY

On the marshlands where wildfowlers once stalked their prey, and on pastures where shepherds heeded their flocks, now stand thousands of modern houses and bungalows. So much of Canvey has been built on that it is surprising to find a parcel of land to delight the naturalist! However, a large area of saltmarsh and grassland at West Canvey Marsh was bought from the supermarket giant Morrisons by the RSPB in 2006. The 640 acre site will be protected as a nature reserve and the habitat improved with irrigation to encourage breeding wading birds such as lapwing and redshank and overwintering wild duck.

HOW TO GET THERE

By road From the A13 near Basildon take the A130 to Canvey Island. The B1014 from South Benfleet also crosses to the island near Benfleet station.
By rail Nearest station is at Benfleet on the London (Fenchurch Street) to Shoeburyness line.

ORDNANCE SURVEY MAPS

Landranger 1:50,000 series No. 178

TOURIST INFORMATION

The nearest tourist information centre is Southend-on-Sea Tourist Information Centre, Southend Pier, Western Esplanade, Southend-on-Sea SS1 1EE (tel. 01702 215120). Website: www.southend.gov.uk

WHERE TO STAY

There is one caravan and campsite and only limited other accommodation on Canvey Island. However, nearby Southend-on-Sea offers a much wider range of hotels and bed and breakfast establishments. For more details contact Southend-on-Sea Tourist Information Centre (see above).

ISLAND WALKS

A footpath follows the sea defence wall from Thorney Bay to Canvey Point, a distance of three miles.

PLACES TO VISIT

● Dutch Cottage Museum
● Castle Point Transport Museum
● Art Deco Labworth Cafe

Below *This flood barrier was built across Benfleet Creek following the disastrous floods that hit Canvey Island in 1953, in which 58 people died and over 10,000 were left homeless. Its three gates can be lowered at times of extreme high tides*

FOULNESS ISLAND

Thanks to its present owner, the Ministry of Defence, Foulness is one of the least visited islands around the coast of England and Wales. For centuries, its flat, fertile farmland was much sought after by farmers for grazing sheep and cattle, while its remoteness from the law also attracted smugglers, horse stealers and bare-knuckled fighters. All this changed when the War Department bought most of the island for weapons testing in 1915. Live firing still takes place, and permission to visit Foulness must first be obtained from the island's managing company, QinetiQ.

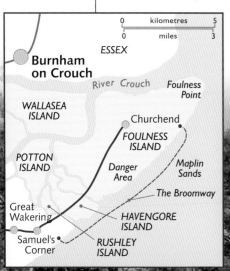

Below *The 17th century George & Dragon in Churchend is the sole pub on Foulness Island and can only be visited by obtaining prior permission from the landlord. Its walled garden was used in the 19th century as an arena for bare-knuckled fighting. Adjacent to the pub are the 19th century church of St Mary and the island's post office.*

HISTORY

For centuries, the island of Foulness was linked to the mainland by an ancient raised track, known as the Broomway, which runs parallel to the shore across the vast expanse of Maplin Sands. Thought by some to date back to the Roman occupation, access along it was only possible a few hours either side of low tide. All this changed in 1922 when the military moved in and built bridges and a road onto the island.

Farming has always been important on Foulness, and its fertile soil has supported arable crops, sheep and cattle since the 13th century, if not before. These rich farmlands were further extended in the early 15th century when a process of land reclamation began - the earliest recorded project of this type in Britain.

THE GEORGE & DRAGON

Until a few years ago there were two pubs on Foulness but the King's Head at Courtsend is now closed. The 17th century timber framed George & Dragon was originally a row of cottages and became an inn in the early 18th century. It became famous during the early 19th century for its illegal bare-knuckled fighting competitions with the local farm bailiff John Bennewith being the island champion for many years. Today, the pub can only be visited by obtaining prior permission from the landlord who will then pass on this information to the QinetiQ security gate over four miles away at Samuel's Corner. Once through the security checkpoint visitors are not allowed to stop on Foulness until they reach the pub. On a sunny summer's day it is well worth a visit!

Foulness, much of it now below sea level, is protected from high tides by an ancient and massive sea wall over 13 miles in length. Over the centuries, however, these sea defences have been breached during periods of extreme high tides. The last such occasion was in 1953, when virtually the whole island was under water for three weeks, and two people and hundreds of farm animals perished in the flood.

A chapel was first established on Foulness in the late 13th century, and was replaced by a timber framed church following the Dissolution of the Monasteries in the mid-16th century. This, in turn, was replaced by the present church of St Mary in 1853. The church, adjacent to the George & Dragon pub, the post office and general stores, form the hub of the island's community in the pleasant village of Churchend.

Military interest in Foulness began in the 19th century when Henry Shrapnel's deadly shell was first test fired on the island. An official military firing range was soon established and by 1915 much of the land, including the 25,000 acres of Maplin Sands, had been bought by the War Department. A plan was even put forward in 1971 to build a third London Airport on 18,000 acres of Maplin Sands, but conservationists, concerned at the damage to the internationally important local bird life, managed to scupper the scheme. Today, apart from the church and a few other buildings, the whole of Foulness is owned by the MOD and is managed for them by QinetiQ. Live firing of shells still takes place and prior permission is required for a visit to this fascinating island.

NATURAL HISTORY

Curiously, MOD control of Foulness and Maplin Sands and the subsequent lack of interference by man has greatly helped to conserve the natural wildlife in this vast expanse of marshland and sandbanks. To the east of the island, Maplin Sands are now an internationally important site for large numbers of wading birds, such as avocet, and overwintering Brent geese, who feed on the dwarf eel grass found in this part of the Thames Estuary. At the northern tip of the island, the large cockleshell banks at Foulness Point are designated a Site of Special Scientific Interest and are home to large numbers of common and little tern, oystercatcher and ringed plover. A rich diversity of plantlife also grows on Foulness, with the marshland behind the sea wall supporting over 200 different species of wild flower. Field trips to Foulness are occasionally organised by local ornithological and wildlife groups.

HOW TO GET THERE

By road from the village of Great Wakering, north of Shoeburyness, to the QinetiQ security gate at Samuel's Corner. Visitors who have prior permission to visit Foulness Island will then drive over four miles to the village of Churchend, where they can visit the George & Dragon pub.

ORDNANCE SURVEY MAPS

Landranger 1:50,000 series No. 178

TOURIST INFORMATION

Southend-on-Sea Tourist Information Centre, Southend Pier, Western Esplanade, Southend-on-Sea SS1 1EE (tel. 01702 215120). Website: www.southend.gov.uk

WHERE TO STAY

The George & Dragon pub in Churchend offers bed and breakfast accommodation. For details contact the landlord (tel. 01702 219460) or visit the pub's website: www.georgeanddragonpub.co.uk For other accommodation on the mainland contact Southend-on-Sea Tourist Information Centre (see above).

WALLASEA ISLAND

The second largest of the Essex islands, Wallasea Island was renowned for centuries for its oysters and its fertile farmland. During the 20th century, nature, in the form of floods, and man, in the form of modern drainage systems, both left their mark on the island and its economy. Today, while the extreme western end of the island is bustling with timber wharves, a marina and a holiday park, the rest of the island is now owned by only one farm. In 2006, part of this farmland was flooded under a government-sponsored scheme to create a wetlands habitat.

HISTORY

Although linked to the mainland by road since the 19th century, Wallasea is still a remote outpost of the Essex archipelago of islands. Famed for its oyster beds from the Roman occupation until their demise during the great tide of 1953, Wallasea Island also once supported seven farms – for many centuries protected by a ten-mile seawall. However, apart from the extreme western end of the island, the remains of the island's historic features and field systems were destroyed during extensive drainage works carried out during the 20th century.

Apart from farming and the now-defunct oyster farms, in the 1920s Wallasea Island also became an important destination for the importing of timber from the Baltic – a practice which still continues today. For over 400 years Wallasea, along with the rest of the Essex coastline, has had its fair share of floods caused by tidal surges in the North Sea. Particularly damaging were the floods of 1736, 1897 and, more recently, in 1953. During the latter floods most of the island was underwater within a very short time, killing two people and hundreds of farm animals.

Today, the extreme western end of the island is not only home to the busy timber wharf, but also to the extensive Essex Marina, a camping and caravan site and the Creeksea Ferry Inn. The rest of the island is now owned by one farm, and a large area of its land was deliberately flooded in 2006 to provide a wetland habitat for wading birds – thus helping to offset areas of mudflat and salt marsh lost to industrial development in other parts of eastern England.

NATURAL HISTORY

Most of Wallasea Island is privately owned and access is restricted. However, with the creation of the government-sponsored Wallasea Wetlands Project and the return of wading birds to the newly formed saltmarshes and mudflats, it is likely that access will be available to the public in the future. On the mainland close to Wallasea Island, the 16-acre Lion Creek Nature Reserve, home to many

Above *Long before they were used to import timber from the Baltic in the 1920s, the wharves on Wallasea Island were busy with seagoing traffic. In the early 19th century a railway was proposed, but never built, to connect them directly to London.*

wading birds and rare species of saltmarsh plant, birds of prey, butterfly and cricket, is owned and managed by the Essex Wildlife Trust.

HOW TO GET THERE
By road By unclassified roads from Ashingdon or Rochford, north of Southend-on-Sea, via Great Stambridge or Canewdon.
By boat A passenger ferry operates from Burnham-on-Crouch to Essex Marina on Wallasea Island during the period from Whitsun to late summer.

ORDNANCE SURVEY MAPS
Landranger 1:50,000 series No. 178

TOURIST INFORMATION
Southend-on-Sea Tourist Information Centre, Southend Pier, Western Esplanade, Southend-on-Sea SS1 1EE (tel. 01702 215120).
Website: www.southend.gov.uk
or Burnham-on-Crouch Community and Tourist Information Centre, The Quay, Burnham-on-Crouch, Essex (tel 01621 784962).
Website: www.maldon.gov.uk

WHERE TO STAY
The Riverside Village Holiday Park on Wallasea Island provides a site for camping and caravans (tel. 01702 258297). For other accommodation in the nearby area contact the Southend-on-Sea Tourist Information Centre (see above).

ISLAND WALKS
Nearly all of Wallasea Island is privately owned by one farm. However there is a

Above *At the western end of Wallasea Island, the Creeksea Ferry Inn, protected from the tidal River Crouch by a seawall, is a popular spot for visiting yachtsmen from the nearby Essex Marina and holidaymakers from the camping and caravan site.*

pleasant stroll to be taken at the western end of the island, from the road across Paglesham Creek along the seawall to the Creeksea Ferry Inn and Essex Marina. A permissive footpath extends the coastal right of way by nearly one mile.

Below *During World War II, fast motor torpedo boats were built for the Royal Navy on Wallasea Island in boatyards that are now home to the Essex Marina. A regular passenger ferry service operates during the summer months from here across the River Crouch to Burnham-on-Crouch.*

NORTHEY ISLAND

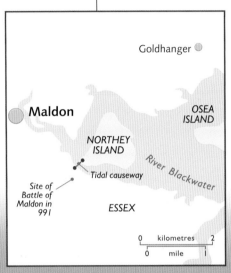

Goldhanger

Maldon

OSEA ISLAND

NORTHEY ISLAND

River Blackwater

Tidal causeway

Site of Battle of Maldon in 991

ESSEX

0 kilometres 2
0 mile 1

L inked to the Essex mainland by a narrow tidal causeway, Northey Island became the springboard for Viking invaders who defeated the English at the nearby Battle of Maldon in 991AD. Later farmed by the monks of Beeleigh Abbey, the island's fertile farmland has been encroached upon by rising sea levels and is now only one-third of its former size. Owned from the 1920s until 1978 by Nobel Peace Prize winner Sir Norman Angell and his descendants, the island is now a nature reserve owned and managed by the National Trust.

Below *When Sir Norman Angell bought Northey Island in the 1920s, he built an eccentric three-storey house that enabled him to have views over the island and its causeway. A circular nature trail around the island's sea wall gives visitors views across the flooded saltmarshes and the Blackwater estuary.*

HISTORY

Located in the River Blackwater estuary close to the town of Maldon, Northey Island and the adjoining mainland is the site of the famous 10th century Battle of Maldon. In 991AD Viking invaders, led by Anlaf, sailed up the River Blackwater in an abortive bid to seize the town of Maldon. Beaten back by the well fortified town's defenders, the Vikings retired to Northey Island to lick their wounds. In the meantime, powerful forces, led by Earldorman Byrhtnoth, arrived to reinforce the English side. At low tide, the Vikings attempted to cross the causeway from the island, but were beaten back by the English. Byrhtnoth eventually allowed the Vikings to cross to the mainland where he thought that he could defeat them. Sadly, Byrhtnoth was killed in the ensuing battle and his head chopped off by the Vikings who took it back to their base on the Isle of Sheppey (see pages 82-85) in Kent.

From the late 12th century, Northey Island was owned by the White Canons of Beeleigh Abbey, near Maldon, who grew wheat on the island's fertile farmland. After the Dissolution of the monasteries in the 16th century, the Abbey and its lands were given to Sir John Gate, the Chancellor of the Duchy of Lancaster.

From the early 18th century onwards, rising sea levels started to threaten Northey Island and many breaches of its outer seawall were left unrepaired. Much of the former farmland reverted to saltmarsh, and less than a third of the island was left protected by the building of an inner seawall.

In the 1920s, Northey Island was sold to the political author, MP and later Nobel Peace Prize winner, Sir Norman Angell. Although his attempt at farming the island was not successful, his legacy today is the strange three-storey house that he built, now used as the home of the resident National Trust warden. After World War II, Northey Island was given by Sir Norman to his nephew Eric Angell Lane who, in 1978, gave it and nearby South House Farm on the mainland to the National Trust.

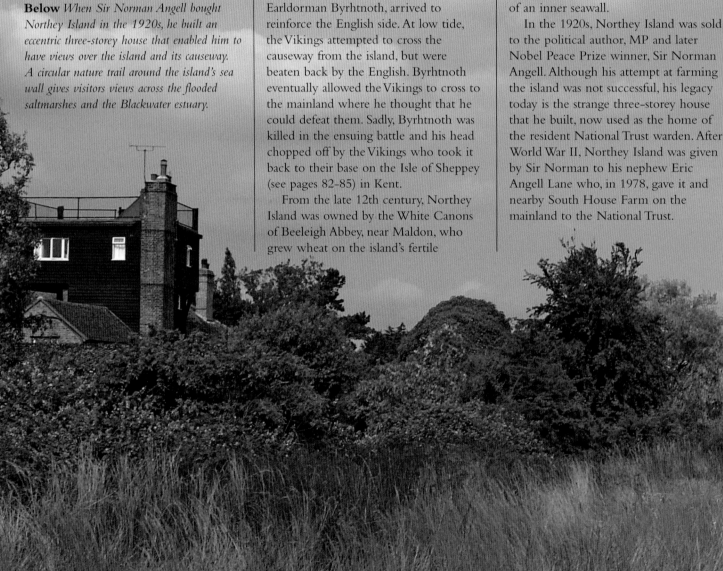

NATURAL HISTORY

Designated as a Site of Special Scientific Interest and owned and managed by the National Trust, the Northey Island nature reserve is an important site for seabirds and rare saltmarsh plantlife. The island is particularly renowned for the large numbers of Brent goose that arrive there during the winter months.

HOW TO GET THERE

From Maldon, take the unclassified road south towards the village of Mundon. About half a mile south of Maldon, turn left along a lane past South House Farm to a small National Trust parking area situated below the sea wall. From here, Northey Island is reached on foot across a tidal causeway. Visitors are reminded that they must first seek permission to visit from the National Trust warden on Northey Island (tel. 01621 853142). No dogs are allowed on the island.

ORDNANCE SURVEY MAPS

Landranger 1:50,000 series No. 168

TOURIST INFORMATION

Maldon Tourist Information Centre, Coach Lane, Maldon, Essex CM9 4UH (tel. 01621 856503).
Website: www.maldon.gov.uk

WHERE TO STAY

There is a wide range of accommodation available in Maldon. For details contact the Maldon Tourist Information Centre (see above).

ISLAND WALK

From the warden's house, a circular footpath follows the sea wall around Northey Island.

Below *Following major breaches to the outer sea wall in the 18th and 19th centuries, over two-thirds of Northey Island reverted to saltmarshes. However, the loss of arable land has since been outweighed by an increease in many rare species of saltmarsh plants*

THAMES' SAILING BARGES

Once a common sight around the coasts and river estuaries of eastern England, there are now only a few Thames sailing barges left in working order. The Blackwater estuary around Northey Island is one of the best locations to see these graceful ships in action. Visitors to Northey Island can also see the wrecked hulk of the *Mistley*, a Thames sailing barge built in Harwich in 1891 to carry wheat.

MERSEA ISLAND

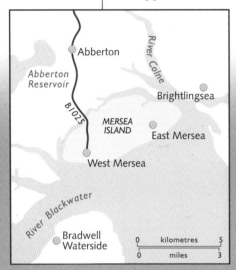

From Roman times to the present day, Mersea Island has been a favourite haunt for those seeking rest and recreation. Strategically located at the mouth of the River Colne and the approaches to Colchester, the peace of this little island has only been seriously interrupted on three occasions – during Viking raids, the English Civil War and World War II. Famed for its oysters, fish restaurants and sailing facilities, Mersea Island is lucky to have escaped the excesses of modern commercialisation.

Below *Clustered around West Mersea's harbour front are several boatyards, the lifeboat station and the West Mersea Yacht Club. Founded in 1899, the club provides sheltered moorings and is one of the foremost centres for sailing on the east coast. The club's flag consists of the red ensign and three scimitars.*

HISTORY

Artefacts found on Mersea Island show that the island been occupied since Stone Age times. However, it was the Romans who left a more enduring mark on this, the most easterly of the inhabited Essex islands. Located only five miles south of the former Roman town of Camulodunum, or Colchester as it is known today, Mersea Island was used as a place of quiet retreat by retired soldiers for rest and recreation. The most visible reminder of their occupation, a large Romano-British burial mound, can be seen in the northwest of the island soon after crossing The Strood causeway. Other, less visible, remains uncovered near West Mersea church include mosaic pavements and a wheel tomb. The

Romans also left behind traces of their salt manufacturing industry and, more importantly, introduced oyster farming – an industry which is still important on the island today. It is also thought likely that The Strood causeway, linking Mersea to the mainland, was originally built by the Romans.

Following the withdrawal of the Romans in the early 5th century, Mersea Island, along with the surrounding mainland, soon became part of the Anglo-Saxon kingdom of Essex. Anglo-Saxon features found in West Mersea church suggest that a chapel may well have been built here as early as the 7th century.

By the 9th century, the whole region had become the target for attack by

WEST MERSEA OYSTERS

Introduced by the Romans, oyster farming is still an important industry on Mersea Island. Susceptible to extremes of weather, the local oyster industry has on two occasions since World War II – the Great Tide of 1953 and the Big Freeze of 1962–63 – been virtually wiped out. New stock was introduced and now Mersea oysters are internationally acclaimed. The beginning of the oyster season is celebrated by the Mersea Seafood Festival, held in September each year. The Colchester Oyster Festival is also held annually at the end of October.

Viking raiders from Denmark. The Vikings were fond of using islands around the coast of England as bases from which to attack the mainland. Local examples of this strategy in the late 9th century included Canvey Island, from which they attempted to attack London, and Northey Island, which culminated in the Battle of Maldon. In the same way, the Vikings probably used Mersea as a base to launch attacks on the important Anglo-Saxon town of Colchester. Peace only prevailed in the region after the Norman conquest of England in the 11th century.

During the 16th century, Mersea Island's stategic position at the mouth of the River Colne and the approaches to Colchester led to it being fortified against foreign invaders. Completed in 1543, a large blockhouse armed with 36 cannon was built at the extreme eastern end of the island. The expected French invasion never came and the fort was disarmed. It saw action during the English Civil War, however, when it was captured by Parliamentarian forces in 1648 during the siege of Colchester. Surprisingly, apart from the Mersea Stone, very little remains of this once important structure.

During the 19th century, grandiose plans were drawn up to build a harbour and dock system at the eastern end of Mersea Island but, like a similarly ill-founded early 20th century scheme to build a railway to the island, it never materialised.

In the 20th century, Mersea Island was used during World War II as a decoy site to lure German bombers away from the naval base across the River Colne at Brightlingsea. Known as Starfish Sites, these decoy towns with fires to simulate bomb hits were the brainchild of Colonel Sir John Turner. The sites were built utilising the deception and mock-up skills used in the making of wartime films by Shepperton Studios. The site at East Mersea was never hit by the enemy, but may well have indirectly saved Brightlingsea and its squadron of minesweepers. Coastal defences were also built along the island's south coast and one concrete building is still in use today as a beach cafe in West Mersea.

Today, as in Roman times, Mersea Island attracts those looking for rest and recreation. A delightful village, West Mersea is the most heavily populated part of the island and its harbourside fish restaurants are a popular destination for visitors. Here, a delightful community of houseboats, with their miniature gardens, contrasts with the nearby quiet rows of bungalows and, just along the coast, row upon row of sought-after beach huts.

Above *Along the West Mersea's harbourside are several fish restaurants, much publicised by TV celebrity chefs, which offer a wide range of local fish and, of course, local oysters.*

Above *Hundreds of wooden beach huts line the shingle beach in West Mersea. Rented out on a long term basis by Colchester Borough Council, they are much sought-after with a long waiting list of applicants.*

Below *In 1989, rows of fenced rectangular enclosures were erected to help arrest erosion of the crumbling cliffs in Cudmore Grove Country Park at the eastern end of Mersea Island. The crumbling cliffs, now home to a colony of sand martin, have yielded up 300,000 year old animal fossils.*

NATURAL HISTORY

The primary attraction for naturalists on Mersea Island is the Cudmore Grove Country Park. Located at the eastern end of the island, the park includes areas of grassland, woodland and a beach. Here, erosion by the sea has exposed a large section of cliff which has yielded up 300,000 year old hippo fossils and a mammoth tusk which can be seen on display at the Colchester Natural History Museum. Adjacent to the park is a nature reserve containing an area of saltmarsh.

Out from the shoreline, the food-rich mudflats of the Colne estuary are an important feeding ground for shelduck, curlew and avocet.

HOW TO GET THERE

By road Take the B1025 south from Colchester and cross to Mersea Island over the causeway known as The Strood. Note that the causeway can be flooded during times of high spring tides.
By boat Between late April and early October, a passenger ferry operates from

the extreme eastern end of Cudmore Grove Country Park, East Mersea, to Point Clear and Brightlingsea on the Essex mainland. Timetable details are available on the ferry website: www.brightlingseaferry.co.uk

ORDNANCE SURVEY MAPS
Landranger 1:50,000 series No. 168

TOURIST INFORMATION
Colchester Visitor Information Centre, 1 Queen Street, Colchester, Essex CO1 2PG (tel. 01206 282920) or visit their website: www.visitcolchester.co.uk

WHERE TO STAY
There are several camping and caravan sites on Mersea Island. For details visit the website: www.mersea-island.com

Mersea Island Vineyard also offers accommodation. For further details visit their website: www.merseawine.com

A further choice of accommodation is also available on the nearby mainland and in Colchester. For details contact Colchester Visitor Information Centre (see above).

ISLAND WALKS
It is possible to walk around most of the coastline of Mersea Island, a distance of just over 10 miles, following the sea wall and beaches. Pleasant strolls can also be taken in Cudmore Grove Country Park at the eastern end of the island.

PLACES TO VISIT
● West Mersea Barrow
● Mersea Island Vineyard
● Cudmore Grove Country Park
● Colchester Oyster Fishery, East Mersea
● Mersea Island Museum, West Mersea

Above *A concrete pill box dating from World War II dominates this low lying headland in the Cudmore Grove Country Park. The Mersea Stone, virtually all that remains of externsive 16th century fortifications, stands close to the water's edge a short distance beyond this point. During the summer months, a passenger ferry operates from here across the Colne estuary to Point Clear and the small port of Brightlingsea.*

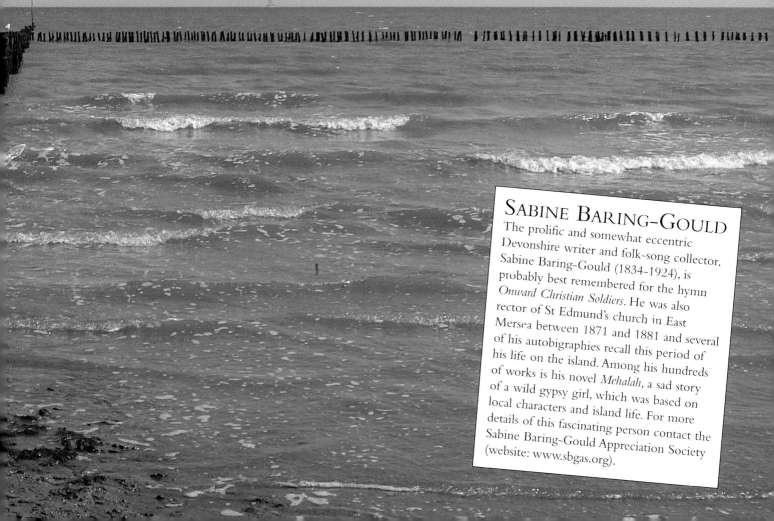

SABINE BARING-GOULD
The prolific and somewhat eccentric Devonshire writer and folk-song collector, Sabine Baring-Gould (1834-1924), is probably best remembered for the hymn *Onward Christian Soldiers*. He was also rector of St Edmund's church in East Mersea between 1871 and 1881 and several of his autobigraphies recall this period of his life on the island. Among his hundreds of works is his novel *Mehalah*, a sad story of a wild gypsy girl, which was based on local characters and island life. For more details of this fascinating person contact the Sabine Baring-Gould Appreciation Society (website: www.sbgas.org).

Below *A paradise for birdwatchers, the barren and remote Farne Islands off the Northumberland coast are now one of the most important nature reserves in Europe. Steeped in the history of the early Christian evangelical monks the Farne Islands, along with Holy Island (or Lindisfarne) to the north, contrast greatly with the windswept flatness and housing estates of Walney Island, off the coast of Cumbria in the north west of England.*

NORTHERN ENGLAND

FARNE ISLANDS
LINDISFARNE
ISLE OF WALNEY

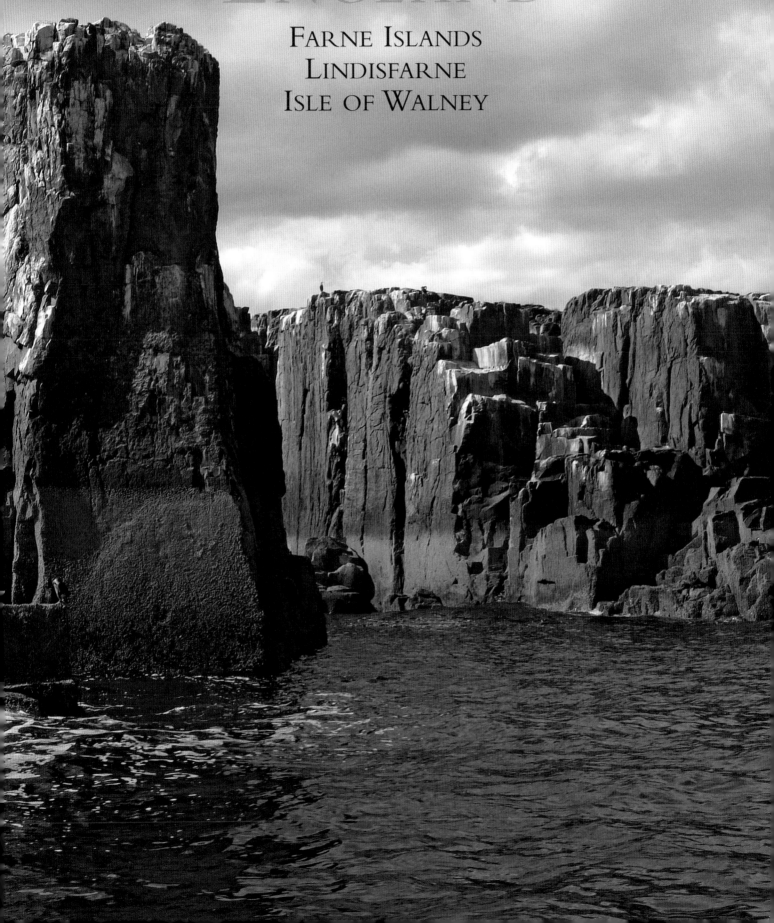

FARNE ISLANDS

Lashed by storms in winter, the solitude and remoteness of the barren Farne Islands attracted hermits and monks from early Christian times. However, by the late 19th century, local concerns about the over-exploitation of the islands' rich natural heritage led them to become one of the world's first bird sanctuaries. Owned by the National Trust since 1925, the Farne Islands, with their vast colonies of protected breeding seabird and grey seal, have become one of the most important nature reserves in Europe.

Above *For centuries, the grey seals of the Farne Islands were killed for their oil and skin. Today, their protected colony is one of the largest in Britain.*

Right *During the nesting season, the dolerite cliffs of Staple Island are home to nearly 20,000 pairs of guillemot. The Farne Islands, especially Staple Island, also attract around 34,000 pairs of nesting puffin!*

HISTORY

For centuries, the remoteness and solitude of the barren Farne Islands attracted early Christian hermits and monks. Written records show that St Aidan, the first bishop of Lindisfarne, spent time in meditation on the islands during the middle of the 7th century . The most famous of local saints, St Cuthbert, retired as Prior of Lindisfarne in 676AD to Inner Farne. Living in a simple stone cell that he built himself, St Cuthbert spent most of his time in meditation on the island until his death in 687AD.

Other hermits continued to live on the Farne Islands until the mid-13th century, when two Benedictine monks and their servants were sent to live on Inner Farne by the Convent of Durham. This small community, known as the House of Farne, was well supported by rich benefactors from the mainland. The monks also grew their own crops, kept livestock and supplemented their income by selling birds' eggs, fish, seals and items salvaged from wrecks. During their stay on Inner Farne, the monks built two chapels, one dedicated to St Mary and the other to St Cuthbert. The present St Cuthbert's Chapel was built around 1370. By the mid-19th century, however, it had become derelict and was only saved by the intervention of the then Archdeacon of Durham. The House of Farne was closed in 1536 during Henry VIII's Dissolution of the Monasteries.

Close to St Cuthbert's Chapel is Castell's Tower, named after the then Prior of Durham, which was erected in the early 16th century. In 1673, the tower became an official lighthouse and a beacon was lit at the top each night.

Lashed by gales and storms during the winter, the Farne Islands had for centuries become a graveyard for ships blown off course onto the treacherous rocks. In addition to the beacon on Inner Farne, stone towers with beacons

Left *The famous Longstone lighthouse on the Outer Farne Islands was opened in 1826. Its first keeper was William Darling who lived there with his family. The lighthouse became automated in 1990.*

GRACE DARLING

TO THE MEMORY OF
GRACE HORSLEY DARLING
A NATIVE OF BAMBURGH
AND AN INHABITANT
OF THESE ISLANDS
WHO DIED OCT* 20*^ A.D. 1842
AGED 26 YEARS.

In 1826, William Darling became the first keeper of the newly opened Longstone lighthouse. Living with him on this inhospitable rock were his wife and youngest daughter, Grace. In September 1838 the *SS Forfarshire*, en route from Hull to Dundee, ran aground on rocks near Longstone. In heavy seas, Grace Darling and her father launched a small rowing boat and rescued nine survivors. For her bravery, Grace became a national heroine. A memorial commemorates her brave deed in St Cuthbert's Chapel on Inner Farne.

were built on Staple Island and on Brownsman during the late 18th century. A modern lighthouse with a revolving beam was first erected on Inner Farne in 1809 by Trinity House and, in 1826, a new lighthouse was opened on Longstone to replace the poorly-situated one on Brownsman.

Following the Dissolution of the Monasteries in 1536, the Farne Islands became the property of the Dean and Chapter of Durham and for the next 300 years were let to tenants who over-exploited the natural resources of the islands. Concerned about the continuing threat to the local seabird population, the Archdeacon of Durham, Charles Thorpe,

purchased the Inner Farne Islands in 1861 and employed men to protect the nests during the important breeding season. Further protection as a bird sanctuary was provided in 1881, with the setting up of the Farne Islands Association. The outer Farne Islands were purchased in 1912 by Lord Armstrong.

The inner and outer Farne Islands were purchased for the National Trust in 1925, and since then have become one of the most important and successful protected seabird breeding grounds and grey seal colonies in Europe.

Left *An excellent way to see the beauty and wildlife of the Farne Islands is to take a boat trip from the harbour at Seahouses. Visitors can land on Inner Farne (left) and Staple Island between April and September.*

along the east coast of Britain. Once killed in large numbers for their skin and oil, their numbers have steadily increased over the years to the current population of around 3,500.

HOW TO GET THERE
Between the months of April and September, several private companies operate boat trips from Seahouses harbour to the Farne Islands. Landing is only possible on Staple Island and Inner Farne. Landing times during the breeding season are restricted to reduce disturbance to nesting seabirds. No dogs are allowed on the islands. A separate landing fee is payable to the National Trust. For opening times contact the National Trust (tel. 01665 720651 or their Infoline: tel. 01665 721099). Website: www.nationaltrust.org.uk

ORDNANCE SURVEY MAPS
Landranger 1:50,000 series No. 75

TOURIST INFORMATION
Berwick-upon-Tweed Tourist Information Centre, 106 Marygate, Berwick-upon-Tweed, TD15 1DT (tel. 01289 330733)
Seahouses (tel. 01665 720884 – seasonal)
Website: www.northumberland.gov.uk

NATURAL HISTORY
Famous for their colonies of breeding seabird and grey seal, the 28 treeless islands that form the Farne Islands have been a wildlife sanctuary for over 125 years. Today, they are one of the foremost nature reserves in the whole of Europe.

The two main groups of the Farne Islands are located in the North Sea between two and five miles off the Northumberland coast. They mainly consist of hard dolerite rock which is ideal for nesting seabirds. Although the islands have little soil, they support a rich variety of plantlife, especially sea

campion, mosses and lichens.

At least 15 species of seabird now successfully breed on the islands, including over 34,000 pairs of puffin. The total number of breeding pairs of shag, guillemot, gull, eider duck and tern exceeds 30,000. Oystercatcher, fulmar and cormorant can also be seen nesting on the islands. Visitors to Inner Farne during June are advised to wear hard hats to protect them from dive-bombing arctic tern!

The Farne Islands also support a large colony of grey seal and are the only breeding ground for these mammals

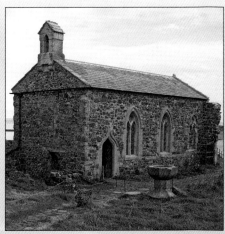

WHERE TO STAY
There is no accommodation on the Farne Islands. For accommodation in Seahouses contact Berwick-upon-Tweed or Seahouses (seasonal) Tourist Centres.

ISLAND WALKS
There are nature trails on both Inner Farne and Staple Island.

PLACES TO VISIT
On Inner Farne:
- St Cuthbert's Chapel
- Grace Darling's memorial
On Staple Island:
- Old beacon lighthouse

Above *Castell's Tower on Inner Farne was completed around 1500 and later used as a fort. A lighthouse with a beacon of fire was established on the top of the tower towards the end of the 17th century.*

Right *St Cuthbert's Chapel on Inner Farne was built in the 14th century. Restored in the 19th century, it also contains a memorial to local heroine Grace Darling.*

Below *Slightly smaller than the cormorant, the shags on the Farne Islands were almost wiped out in 1968 from eating poisoned fish. Since then their numbers have increased to over 1,000 pairs.*

HOLY ISLAND
LINDISFARNE

Holy Island, or Lindisfarne, is one of the most important religious sites in Britain. From the 7th century AD, evangelical missionaries travelled far and wide from their island base to convert the mainland pagan population. Driven out by the Vikings, they rebuilt their religious community on the island in Norman times until they were suppressed in the 16th century by Henry VIII. Small scale industrialisation during the 19th century did not last but, since then, the island has become a mecca for pilgrims, tourists and ornithologists.

HISTORY

In 634AD, King Oswald of Northumbria ruled his kingdom from Bamburgh Castle. Recently converted to Christianity, Oswald sent to the island of Iona for a missionary to convert his pagan subjects. The first missionary, named Corman, was unsuccessful and returned to Iona. However, in 635AD, a group of monks led by his successor, Aidan, settled on Lindisfarne where they built a monastery and were soon successful in converting the Northumbrian people to the new faith. For the next 250 years, the religious community on Lindisfarne flourished. They were highly influential in the spread of Christianity across Britain, sending out missionaries, teaching, and producing beautifully illuminated manuscripts. Probably the most revered Bishop of Lindisfarne was Cuthbert who reigned for only two years until 687AD. His body, along with important early Christian relics, was finally laid to rest in Durham Cathedral in 1070.

From 793AD, the peaceful idyll of the monks' life on Lindisfarne came under attack from Viking invaders. In 875AD, the

Left *The present causeway to Holy Island was opened in 1954 and can be crossed by vehicles at low tide. Half way across the causeway a refuge tower provides safety for unwary travellers caught out by the fast rising tides.*

Above *For centuries, the harbour at Holy Island was an important centre for the herring fishing industry. Employing many local people, the industry had gone into terminal decline by the end of the 19th century due to the growth of mainland ports and their accessibility by railways.*

Below *Until the causeway to Holy Island was opened in 1954, travellers had to cross the treacherous sands at low tide on foot or by pony and cart. This line of poles, known as the Pilgrim's Way, marks the centuries-old direct route from the mainland to the island.*

monks fled to the mainland, taking with them holy relics, St Cuthbert's body and the famous Lindisfarne Gospels. These beautiful manuscripts were written by Bishop Eadfrid of Lindisfarne and now reside in the British Library in London.

Peace did not return to Lindisfarne until after the Norman Conquest of 1066 and, in 1082, the Bishop of Durham allowed Benedictine monks to return to the island. It was about this time that the name of Lindisfarne was changed to Holy Island. By the early 12th century they had rebuilt the ruined priory and built St Mary's Church. In the intervening years until the Dissolution of Monasteries, the monks of Holy Island led an uneventful life.

When Henry VIII closed the monastery in 1537, the island became a military base in the fight against the Scots. By 1550, the priory buildings had been destroyed to supply stone for the building of a new castle.

Changing hands during the English Civil War, Lindisfarne Castle remained a military stronghold until 1820 and, in 1880, was bought by Edward Hudson, the owner of *Country Life* magazine. It was later restored as a residence for Hudson

by Sir Edwin Lutyens. In 1944, the castle was given to the National Trust.

Industry was once an important source of employment on the island. As early as the 14th century, the monks had started quarrying limestone and mining coal. During the 17th century, iron ore was also mined on the island and shipped to iron works in Scotland. The limestone industry was greatly expanded in the mid-19th century when lime kilns, horse drawn waggonways and a jetty were built. However, along with the once-important herring fishing industry, this had all but disappeared by 1900.

Since then, Holy Island has become increasingly dependent on tourism, with thousands of visitors and pilgrims each year attracted by its unique religious history and the recent revival of Celtic Christianity.

NATURAL HISTORY

A large part of Holy island is now a national nature reserve managed by English Nature. The area has a wealth of important habitats, including tidal mudflats rich in food sources, saltmarshes with diverse plant communities and sand dunes stabilised by marram grass.

In turn, these habitats create an important source of food and protection for the visiting bird population, especially during the winter when thousands of

waders and wildfowl descend on the island. Most important are the Brent goose which arrives every autumn from Spitzbergen, along with greylag and pinkfooted goose, grey plover, bar-tailed godwit and widgeon. Also attracted are thousands of birdwatchers who arrive to enjoy the spectacle of this internationally important gathering. Migrating birds, including finch, thrush and warbler also pass through Holy Island in the spring and autumn.

HOW TO GET THERE

From the A1 south of Berwick-upon-Tweed at West Mains an unclassified road crosses to Holy Island across a three mile tidal causeway. Tide timetables are displayed at each end of the causeway and should be consulted before crossing to or from the island. Tide timetables are also available on the following website: www.northumberlandlife.org/holy-island/

ORDNANCE SURVEY MAPS

Landranger 1:50,000 series No. 75

Below *Lindisfarne Castle, built on a volcanic dolerite intrusion, watches over the old upturned herring boats beached above the harbour. All that now remains of this once-important industry is a small number of shellfishing boats.*

TOURIST INFORMATION
Berwick-upon-Tweed Tourist
Information Centre, 106 Marygate,
Berwick-upon-Tweed, TD15 1DT
(tel. 01289 330733)
Website: www.northumberland.gov.uk

WHERE TO STAY
There are two hotels, two inns and
several bed and breakfast establishments
on Holy Island. For further details visit
the island's website: www.lindisfarne.org.uk
or contact Berwick-upon-Tweed Tourist
Information Centre (see above).

ISLAND WALKS
A circular walk is possible, partly
following the route of an old 19th
century waggonway built for the
limestone industry. From the village, the
route takes in views of the harbour and
castle, the east coast of the island and the
site of disused lime quarries before
returning across The Links to the village.

PLACES TO VISIT
● Ruins of Priory (English Heritage)
● 12th century St Mary's Church
● Lindisfarne Castle (National Trust)
● Limekilns at Castle Point
● Lindisfarne Heritage Centre
● St Cuthbert's Isle (on foot at low tide)
● Lindisfarne National Nature Reserve
(English Nature)

Above *In 1860, a Scottish company greatly
expanded the limestone quarrying industry on
Holy Island. They constructed lime kilns, seen
above near the castle, waggonways and a jetty.
This ambitious venture had closed by 1900.*

Right *Destroyed by Henry VIII for its stone
to build the nearby castle, the gaunt ruins of
the Benedictine Priory on Holy Island are
now in the care of English Heritage.*

ISLE OF WALNEY

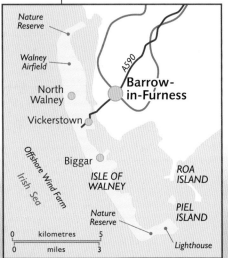

irst farmed by the Cistercian monks of Furness Abbey, the low-lying Isle of Walney has witnessed many changes over the last 700 years. The 17th century witnessed both bubonic plague and the upheaval of the English Civil War, and by the 20th century the face of Walney had dramatically changed. A planned housing estate for shipyard workers and the construction of a bridge to the mainland were soon followed by airship building and a military airfield. Today, apart from its large housing estates, Walney is also home to two important nature reserves.

HISTORY

Artefacts which have been discovered in the north of the island, in the form of flint tools and weapons, show that Walney has been inhabited since the Stone Age. By the 12th century, the Cistercian Savignac monks of Furness Abbey, near Dalton-in Furness on the nearby mainland, were farming on the island and this continued until the Dissolution of Monasteries in 1536.

The 17th century brought much misery to the people of Walney and the Furness region. In 1631, half of the population of Walney was wiped out in an outbreak of bubonic plague. Later, during the English Civil War (1642-1651), the strongly Parliamentarian Furness area was the scene of several bitter battles with Royalist forces. For a while, the Parliamentarian fleet was anchored between Walney Island and nearby Piel Island. In 1644, Royalist forces attacked the village of North Scale in the northeast of the island, and burned it to the ground.

For centuries, farming and fishing had been the main occupation of the people of Walney. This all changed in the late 19th century when salt extraction began on the island. At this time, the shipyard at Barrow-in-Furness was expanding and more houses were needed for its workers. The Isle of Walney Estates Company was formed in 1898 to build an estate on the island for shipyard workers. A year later, the company was taken over by the shipyard's owners, Vickers, and by 1904 when the estate - known as Vickerstown - was completed, a total of nearly 1,000 new homes had been built. Vickerstown was enlarged during the late 1930s and designated a conservation area in 1988.

The narrow Walney Channel had always separated the island from Barrow-in-Furness and was crossed by a ferry. To improve communications for the vastly increased population on Walney, a toll bridge was opened between Vickerstown and Barrow in 1908. Now known as Jubilee Bridge, the tolls across it were abolished in 1935.

In 1913, an enormous shed was built by Vickers in North Walney to house the construction of airships. Measuring over

Below *Nearly 10 miles long, the sand and shingle beach of the Isle of Walney's west coast is constantly buffeted by the Irish Sea. Four miles out to sea is this large wind farm which was completed in the Spring of 2006. Its 30 turbines generate enough electricity for over 80,000 homes in the Furness region. The Isle of Walney was used by the Rev W Awdry as the location for the Island of Sodor in his* Thomas the Tank Engine *children's books.*

500ft long and nearly 100ft high, the shed was used to build airships during World War I. The final airship to be built here was the famous R80 which was completed in 1921. During World War I, the Walney airship shed was shelled by the German U-boat, U21. Fire was returned by the guns on Walney Fort and no damage was inflicted on the shed.

During World War II, an airfield was constructed for the RAF at the north end of Walney. A large camp grew up around the airfield which, until it closed in 1946, was used by the RAF as an air gunnery school.

NATURAL HISTORY

At its highest point, low-lying Walney is only 50ft above sea level. To the north are large areas of sand dune, saltmarsh and heathland. The southern tip of the island, formed from a sand spit, contains areas of saltmarsh and is surrounded by sand and mudflats.

In recent years, both the northern and southern ends of Walney have been designated as nature reserves and, as such, are managed by the Cumbria Wildlife Trust. The North Walney Reserve is an important site for the rare natterjack toad, rare plants, butterflies and moths. The South Walney Reserve has a bird observatory, where visitors can see one of the largest colonies of greater and lesser black-backed gull in Europe. In addition to gulls, the reserve is an important site for eider duck, common and little tern, oystercatcher and shelduck. During the winter, the reserve is visited by thousands of wildfowl and wading birds.

HOW TO GET THERE
By road take the A590 from Barrow-in-Furness across Jubilee Bridge to Vickerstown on the Isle of Walney.

ORDNANCE SURVEY MAPS
Landranger 1:50,000 series No. 96

TOURIST INFORMATION
Barrow-in-Furness Tourist Information Centre, Forum 28, 28 Duke Street, Barrow-in-Furness LA14 1HU (tel. 01229 894784) or visit the website: www.lakelandgateway.info

WHERE TO STAY
There is a wide range of accommodation in nearby Barrow-in-Furness and the surrounding Furness area. For details contact the Barrow-in-Furness Tourist

Above *Vickerstown was built by Vickers in the early 20th century as a housing estate for its workers in the Barrow shipyards. Later extended in the 1930s, its wide streets and solid houses are overlooked by the enormous erecting sheds in Barrow where, today, Britain's nuclear submarines are built.*

Information Centre (see above). There is also a caravan park at South End on Walney Island.

ISLAND WALKS
There are a series of nature trails in the South Walney Nature Reserve.

PLACES TO VISIT
● South Walney Nature Reserve
● North Walney Nature Reserve
● Piel Island (via Barrow-in-Furness)

PIEL ISLAND
Located a short distance from the southern tip of Walney, little Piel Island has had a fascinating history. Between the 12th century and the Dissolution of the Monasteries in 1536, the island was owned by the Cistercian monks of Furness Abbey and used by them as a harbour for importing goods. Warehouses were built and, in the 14th century, the island was fortified to protect it against pirates. During the English Civil War, the Parliamentarian navy sheltered for a while in Piel Harbour. The harbour continued to be used up until the 19th century, and excise men were based here to fight the illegal activities of smugglers. The island was lovingly recalled in a poem by Wordsworth after he visited there in 1805. Today Piel Island, with its ruined castle and old cottages, is ruled over by the landlord of the 18th century Ship Inn - otherwise known as the King of Piel!

How to get to Piel Island: Take the A5087 from Barrow-in-Furness to Rampside. From here follow the causeway to Roa Island, where a small passenger ferry departs for Piel Island during the summer months.

114

Below *Looking north from the slopes of
North Barrule, the lowland region of the Isle
of Man stretches to its most northerly point at
the Point of Ayre. The harbour town of
Ramsey, on the right, shot to fame when it
was visited by Queen Victoria and Prince
Albert in 1847. Now, each June, the roads
around the town and through the surrounding
hills are part of the 37-mile circuit for
motorcycles during the internationally famous
Isle of Man TT races.*

ISLE OF MAN

ISLE OF MAN

Located in the Irish Sea, midway between Scotland, England and Ireland, the Isle of Man is a self-governing Crown dependency and a member of the British Commonwealth. The island's rock formations, formed over 500 million years ago, are responsible for its rugged coastline and hilly interior, and its climate is tempered by the warming effects of the Gulf Stream. Inhabited since the Stone Age, the Isle of Man and its fiercely independent people have a rich historical and cultural past. The Celts, early Christians, Vikings, Scots and English have all left their mark on this unique island and, today, their legacy sits comfortably alongside international banking and prosperity.

Point of Ayre

Irish Sea

Ramsey

Kirkmichael

Laxey Wheel

Snaefell

Manx Electric Railway

ISLE OF MAN

Peel

Snaefell Mountain Railway

Laxey

Isle of Man Railway

Douglas

Ballasalla

Port Erin

Ronaldsway Airport

Port St Mary

Castletown

Calf of Man

| 0 | kilometres | 10 |
| 0 | miles | 6 |

Below *Once a thriving fishing port and a centre for smuggling in the 18th century, historic Peel still retains its individuality. Its narrow streets and old fishing sheds now rub shoulders with the modern yachts in the harbour.*

HISTORY

Flint tools, used by hunters and fishermen from the Middle Stone Age, have been discovered on the Isle of Man and show that the island has been inhabited for at least 7,000 years. More advanced people, with skills in farming and pottery, settled on the island from about 4000BC. Their burial sites, marked by large standing stones or megaliths, can be seen at several locations on the island today. In particular, the Neolithic burial

site at Maughold just south of Ramsey, is one of the largest in the British Isles. From about 1800BC to 500BC, the Isle of Man's trading links and rich natural resources helped it to become an important centre for the manufacture of bronze artefacts. Then, around 500BC, the Celts arrived on the island and ushered in a new age of culture and prosperity.

The Celts left a rich legacy on the Isle of Man. They not only brought their music, art and language to the island, but they also left behind substantial remains of their roundhouses, farms and forts. A large Celtic hillfort and hut circles can be seen today on the summit of South Barrule in the south of the island. The Celts also excelled in making jewellery and pottery and in spinning and weaving, and developed trading links with the rest of the known world. Ignored by the Romans, these Celts were eventually converted to Christianity by early missionaries from Ireland and Scotland around 600AD. The remains of many early Christian chapels and elaborately

Above *A microcosm of Manx history, St Patrick's Isle has been inhabited for at least 7,000 years and is now connected to Peel by a causeway. St Patrick's church, Peel Castle and St German's cathedral all stand testimony to Man's importance to the early Christians and later, Viking, Scots and English rulers.*

carved crosses from this period can be seen in many locations on the island today. The Celts continued to live peacefully on the island until the end of the 8th century, when the Vikings arrived

Above *Ramsey's rapid growth as a tourist resort during the 19th century was no doubt helped by a visit made there by Queen Victoria and Prince Albert in 1847. Stretching nearly half a mile into Ramsey Bay, Queen's Pier was opened in 1886 and was used for some years by ferries from the mainland. Now disused and forlorn, its cast iron supports show the ravages of nature and time.*

from Norway in their longships.

The Norse rule of the Isle of Man lasted over 400 years and they left behind an enduring cultural and administrative legacy. Soon converted to Christianity, they introduced their own literature, folklore and art. The Norsemen were skilled metalworkers and made elaborately decorated shields and weapons, while their artists produced intricate carvings in wood and stone.

Using the island as their base, the Norsemen set out to conquer lands around the Irish Sea and Scottish islands further north. Eventually all of these possessions became known as the Kingdom of Mann and the Isles. To rule this far-flung kingdom, the Norse established the island's first parliament, the Tynwald, in 979AD. The Tynwald has survived since then and is the oldest continuous parliament in the world.

The Tynwald, Norse for 'meeting place', now consists of a lower chamber of 24 elected members or Keys, and an upper chamber called the Legislative Council. This is made up of three members - the Lord Bishop of Sodor and Man, the attorney general and the President of Tynwald. On 5th July each year new laws are proclaimed at an open-air assembly on Tynwald Hill in St John's.

Following the disintegration of the Norse kingdom in the 13th century, the Isle of Man came under Scottish control. This was not only resented by the Manx people but also by the English who saw

THE GREAT LAXEY WHEEL

Minerals have been mined on the Isle of Man since the 13th century when silver was first extracted. By the mid-19th century, the mining industry on the island had greatly expanded and huge amounts of zinc ore were being extracted from the mine at Laxey. As the mine workings became deeper, however, they became more prone to flooding. To solve this problem, the giant Laxey Wheel was built in 1854 to pump water from the mine. A superb piece of Victorian engineering, the 77ft diameter cast-iron water wheel was named 'Lady Isabella' after the wife of the island's then governor. Powered by water stored high in the hills and fed to the wheel by a series of channels and a reservoir, the wheel remained in operation until the mine closed in 1929. Purchased in 1965 by the Manx Government, the Great Laxey Wheel has now been restored to working order and is one of the major tourist attractions on the island.

the island as an important strategic base. After years of instability, the island finally came under English control in the 14th century after the Scots were defeated by Henry III. However, it was not until the early 15th century that the Isle of Man entered a long period of stability. In the intervening years, the church had virtually appointed itself as a despotic ruler, levying taxes on the Manx people and seizing large amounts of land.

To put an end to the church's greed, Henry VI granted the Isle of Man to two English noblemen, Sir William and Sir John Stanley. The Stanleys, who became the Earls of Derby in 1485, ruled the island until 1735. The only interruption was during the English Civil War, when William Christian led a short-lived Manx uprising, which ended when the monarchy was restored in England.

From 1735, the lordship of the Isle of Man passed to the Duke of Atholl. During his rule, the Manx Bill of Rights was introduced, which gave all Manx people the right to trial by jury and gave the Tynwald the powers to take control of customs duties. These taxes were fixed

at a much much lower rate than in England and soon the island had become a haven for smugglers. However, in 1765, the British government tried to stem this trade by bringing the island under the control of the British Crown. The Dukes of Atholl were compensated for their loss and English customs officers moved in with punitive measures. Although the British Crown was successful in stamping

Above *Ramsey's busy harbour still sees the comings and goings of fishing vessels and coasters. The cast-iron swing bridge was built across the harbour in 1892.*

Below *The backbone of the island's moorland interior is formed by a range of hills, many of which reach over 1,500ft, that strtetch for 21 miles from Ramsey to Port Erin. Sulby Reservoir (below) nestles in a valley to the west of the island's only mountain, Snaefell.*

out the smuggling trade, the Manx people had lost a lucrative income. Poverty on the island became widespread and many Manx people emigrated to find a new life in America.

However, by the early 19th century when ferry services started to operate from mainland England, the local economy slowly began to improve. Swollen by an influx of retired civil servants from the mainland, the population began to increase and, following royal patronage by Queen Victoria, the Isle of Man became an increasingly popular destination for summer tourists. The regular ferry crossings from Liverpool also encouraged thousand of English workers and their

Below *Douglas, now the capital and administrative centre of the Isle of Man, was developed into a thriving resort during the 19th century. More recently, the island's low rates of taxation and government incentives have attracted international banking and investment companies to the town. As a contrast to this modernity, Douglas's Victorian promenade still witnesses the slow progress of horse-drawn trams introduced in 1876.*

familes to spend their holidays on the island. In 1863, important electoral reforms introduced by the House of Keys were approved by the Crown. This gave the Manx people more autonomy in spending locally raised revenue to improve transport, agriculture and education. Attracted by this stability, optimistic Victorian investors poured into the island, building hotels and railways. These projects, along with new mineral mining ventures, drastically improved the employment prospects of the islanders.

Tourism, greatly enhanced by the famous Isle of Man TT races introduced in 1907, also continued to grow during this period with annual visitor figures reaching half a million by the 1930s. Although the tourist trade is still a vital part of the local economy, other business sectors, particularly international banking and investment, are playing an increasingly important role in the Isle of Man's economy.

During the 20th century, the Tynwald increased its powers and today has complete control over its financial and internal affairs. The Isle of Man is now a self-governing Crown dependency with

its own parliament, administrative system and laws. Wealthy residents are attracted by its low taxes and lack of inheritance or capital-gains taxes.

For an island steeped in such a rich historical culture, there has recently been a welcome upsurge in the revival of the Manx language. The unique Manx Gaelic language, which had practically died out on the island by the 19th century, is now taught in schools on the island.

NATURAL HISTORY

With an equable climate, the Isle of Man contains a wide range of habitats, ranging from mountain, moorland, pasture and glen to cliffs, wetlands and beaches. Within each of these habitats there is an wide variety of plant, animal and bird life.

To help protect the island's rich natural beauty, plant and wildlife, the Manx National Heritage and the Manx Wildlife Trust both manage large tracts of land along the coastline and inland.

In the north of the island, an area of dry heathland at The Ayres is an important site for many species of bird, wildflower and butterfly. On the east coast, Maughold Head contains the largest

cormorant colony on the island. Still on the east coast, near Onchan, the Chasms and Sugarloaf are home to large numbers of stonechat, chough, raven, kittiwake and guillemot. In the northwest, near Ballaugh, the Close Sartfield reserve is probably the most spectacular on the island. During the summer, the wildflower meadows are thick with colourful wild orchid and, during the winter, it is home to the largest winter roost of hen harrier in western Europe. In the southwest, Glen Rushen supports a wide range of birdlife, from hen harrier, peregrine and merlin to short-eared owl, redpoll and red grouse.

At the southern tip of the Isle of Man is the Calf of Man. Separated from the main island by a short stretch of water known as Calf Sound, this small rugged 600 acre island is now a bird sanctuary owned by the Manx National Trust. A disused farmouse on The Calf is now a Bird Observatory with a resident warden. Visitors to the Calf of Man can see a wide variety of wildlife, from grey seal, large colonies of seabird and migrants to resident birds such as the chough, raven and stonechat, and the unique

Above *The narrow gauge Isle of Man Railway was opened in stages between 1873 and 1879 and did much to help the development of the island. Radiating out from Douglas, seen above, the lines to Peel, Ramsey and Port Erin were all closed in 1965. A privately-funded and partially successful attempt was made to reopen the railway in 1967, but by the following year the lines to Peel and Ramsey had finally closed. Under private ownership and with support from railway enthusiasts, the line to Port Erin soldiered on. Nationalised since 1976, the steam-operated line from Douglas to Port Erin still remains in operation and its future seems assured.*

MANX ELECTRIC RAILWAY

During the height of the Victorian tourist boom on the Isle of Man a unique and, at that time, technologically advanced electric railway was built northwards from Douglas following the beautiful and rugged coastline to the port of Ramsey. Opened in stages between 1893 and 1899, with a branch to the summit of the island's only mountain Snaefell (2,036ft above sea level), the line became an instant success with visitors. This scenic railway with its unique American-style trams was saved from closure in 1957 when it was nationalised by the Manx government. With much of the rolling stock still in its original form a trip on this historic line is like a trip back in time!

The Manx Wildlife Trust manages 20 nature reserves, of which 17 are open to the public. For full details of these nature reserves contact the Manx Wildlife Trust (tel. 01624 801985) or visit their website: www.wildlifetrust.org.uk/manxwt/

Finally, and unique to the Isle of Man, are its delightfully secretive, wooded glens. Found both inland and on the coast, their lush vegetation and tumbling streams and waterfalls make them a paradise for wildlife. A total of 17 national glens are managed by the Isle of Man Forestry Department and are accessible to the public.

HOW TO GET THERE
By air There are direct flights to Ronaldsway Airport from many airports in the UK and the Republic of Ireland.
By sea Car and passenger ferry services from Liverpool, Heysham, Belfast and Dublin are operated by the Isle of Man Steam Packet Company (tel. 08705 523 523). Website: www.steam-packet.com

ORDNANCE SURVEY MAPS
Landranger 1:50,000 series No. 95

Above *Castletown, once home to the Manx parliament and former capital of the island, is dominated by Castle Rushen. The oldest part of the castle, a square, stone keep, was built by the Norse king of Mann, Godfred II, in the 12th century. Its famous one-fingered clock was donated by Queen Elizabeth I.*

Loaghtan sheep. A birdwatchers' paradise, the Calf is also visited by many rare birds including osprey, red kite and aquatic warbler. In summer, dolphin, porpoise and huge basking shark can be seen offshore. Boat trips operate during the summer months from Port Erin.

TOURIST INFORMATION

There are Tourist Information Centres in all of the main towns, at the airport and at Douglas Sea Terminal. For more details contact Isle of Man Tourist Information Centre (tel. 01624 686766).
Website: www.isleofman.com

WHERE TO STAY

There is a wide range of accommodation on the Isle of Man. For details contact Isle of Man Tourist Information Centre (see above).

ISLAND WALKS

With its rugged coastline and upland interior, the Isle of Man offers many opportunities for walking. There are four designated long distance paths:
1. The Raad ny Foillan, Way of the Gull, is a 96 mile coastal footpath.
2. The Millennium Way is a 28 mile footpath along the centre of the island, from Castletown in the south to Ramsey in the north.

3. Bayr ny Skeddan, or the Herring Way, is a 14 mile path between Castletown and Peel.
4. The Heritage Trail is a 10 mile path along the disused trackbed of the Douglas to Peel railway.

PLACES TO VISIT

● Snaefell Mountain Railway
● Manx Electric Railway
● Victorian steam railway
● Douglas Horse Tramway
● Groudle Glen Railway
    ● Laxey Wheel
      ● Tynwald Hill
        ● Peel Castle

Above *Originally a small fishing village, Port Erin on the southwest coast was developed as seaside resort during the 19th century. Now modern apartments overlook the old lighthouse, tearooms and the sandy beach.*

● Castle Rushen
● Calf of Man bird sanctuary
● Peel Castle and Cathedral
● Celtic and Viking crosses in Maughold churchyard

Below *Just south of Douglas, the little cove at Port Soderick was once thronged with thousands of summer visitors. Now all that remain are rusting relics of its Victorian past and more recent unsuccessful ventures. An electric tramway once ran along the distant clifftops on the Marine Drive back to Douglas. All this is now gone.*

Below By far the largest of the Welsh islands, Anglesey is separated from the mainland by the narrow and turbulent Menai Strait. This sylvan scene, just north of Thomas Telford's famous Menai Bridge, was once the setting for the invasion of the island by the Romans and their bloody victory over the local Celts nearly 2,000 years ago. In comparison, all of the other Welsh islands are fairly small but, despite their size, not only offer the visitor peace and solitude but also a rich diversity of wildlife, natural beauty and history.

WALES

Anglesey
Holy Island
Bardsey Island
Ramsey Island
Skomer Island
Caldey Island
Flat Holm

ANGLESEY

Occupied since the Stone Age, the Isle of Anglesey became one of the last strongholds of the Celts in Britain until being seized by the Romans in the 1st century AD. Following Roman withdrawal, Anglesey became part of the Welsh kingdom of Gwynedd for the next 800 years. The English took over at the end of the 13th century and peace and prosperity eventually returned. Today, the island's 100-mile long coastline - designated an Area of Outstanding Natural Beauty - and its many historic sites have made tourism the major economic activity.

Below *Once the capital of Anglesey, Beaumaris is located at the northern end of the Menai Strait with magnificent views across the water to Snowdonia. The town - its name means 'beautiful marsh' in French - and its castle were built by Edward I in the late 13th century. In addition to the castle, Beaumaris contains many fine pieces of architecture such as the seafront Victoria Terrace. which was designed by the inventor and architect Joseph Hansom in the mid-19th century.*

HISTORY

Flint tools found on the island show that Anglesey has been occupied by humans for the last 10,000 years. These hunter-gatherers gradually developed farming techniques, but little evidence has been found of this on the island. However, these people left their mark in the shape of the huge megalithic burial chambers that can be seen today on Anglesey. Dating from about 3000BC, the best examples are at Bryn Celli Ddu, about two miles southwest of Llanfairpwll, and at Barclodiad y Gawres, located on the clifftops just over a mile south of Rhosneigr. Remains from the Bronze Age (about 1500BC) have also been found on Anglesey, when it is likely that the huge copper ore deposits on Parys Mountain, just over a mile south of

Amlwch, were first excavated.

During the Iron Age and prior to the Roman invasion of Britain, Anglesey was inhabited by the Celts. In addition to remains of their settlements, the most exciting discovery found on Anglesey from this period is the Llyn Cerrig Bach hoard, which was unearthed when the runway for the RAF station at Valley was being built during World War II. Over 150 items were found, including beautifully decorated bronze work, iron tools and weapons and sets of iron manacles used to secure prisoners. Many of these can be seen today in the National Museum of Wales in Cardiff.

Following their invasion of Britain in 43AD, the Romans swiftly moved to subdue the rebellious Celtic tribes throughout the land. Anglesey and Holy

Island became one of their last strongholds, but by 60AD the Romans had reached the Menai Strait. Although the ensuing bloody battle was a great Roman victory, their hold on Anglesey was short-lived. Boudicca's revolt in southern England led to the Roman forces on the island being temporarily withdrawn. It was not until 78AD that a Roman army led by Agricola finally defeated the Celts on Anglesey.

For the next 300 years, the people of Anglesey led a fairly peaceful existence alongside their Roman rulers. Farms prospered on the island and remains of one of these can be seen today at Din Lligwy, about a mile inland from the east coast at Moelfre. The huge copper deposits on Parys Mountain, a mile inland from Amlwch, were certainly mined by the Romans during their time on Anglesey. Stamped copper ingots from this period can be seen today at the National Museum for Wales in Cardiff.

Following the Roman withdrawal from Anglesey in the late 4th century,

Above *Edward I of England chose Beaumaris as the site for the last of his 'Iron Ring' of North Wales' castles in the 13th century. Before building work started, he evicted the local population to Newborough in the south of Anglesey. Designed by the military architect James of St George, the castle's four lines of defensive walls would have made it virtually impregnable to attack. Employing 2,500 craftsmen and builders, construction started in 1295 but was never completed due to lack of funds. Now open to the public, Beaumaris Castle is designated a World Heritage Site.*

Above *Located close to the old monastic buildings at Penmon, this massive stone dovecote was built by Sir Richard Bulkeley at the beginning of the 17th century to provide meat for his estate.*

Right *North of Penmon, Trwyn Du lighthouse was built in 1838 after the wreck of the* Rothesay Castle *on nearby Puffin Island. The lighthouse became unmanned in 1922 and was converted to solar power in 1996. The hypnotic sound of its fog bell is heard once every 30 seconds.*

the island was subjected to raids from Irish pirates who eventually settled on the island. They, in turn, were driven out by a north British warlord called Cunedda in the late 5th century.

Peace settled on the island again and early Christian monks, led by St Seiriol, founded a monastery at Penmon and nearby Puffin Island, in the northeast of Anglesey, during the 6th century. However, the monks' peaceful existence was interrupted by the arrival of Viking raiders on Anglesey during the 9th and 10th centuries.

The arrival of Cunedda in the 5th century led to the foundation of the kingdom of Gwynedd in northwest Wales. Despite Viking incursions during the 9th and 10th centuries and short-lived Norman control, the kingdom remained a powerful force to be reckoned with until it was defeated by the English king, Edward I, in 1283.

The people of Gwynedd did not take this lightly and over the ensuing years there were many rebellions against the English rulers. Edward tried to take control of this part of Wales and built a series of castles along its coastline.

The last castle to be built was at Beaumaris on Anglesey. Building started in 1295, but it was never finished due to lack of funds and building materials. Uprisings against the English rulers continued on Anglesey until the early 15th century, when peace finally settled on the island.

A period of prosperity now ensued, and links between Anglesey and the English throne were firmly cemented when Owain Tudor, born at Plas Penmynydd in Anglesey in 1400, secretly married the widow of the English king, Henry V in 1429. This marriage, and the subsequent three male offspring, eventually gave rise to the Tudor dynasty. Until the Dissolution of the Monasteries under Henry VIII in 1536, the Church also prospered on Anglesey and, with the financial assistance of wealthy English patrons, many new churches were built.

Farming has always been important on low-lying Anglesey and for centuries, the island was known as 'the bread basket of Wales'. However, both the climate and disease had a major impact on the fortunes of Anglesey. Between the 14th and 18th centuries, a mini ice-age over Europe brought lower temperatures and higher precipitation to the island. This, coupled with a drop in population caused by the Black Death, forced farmers to change from labour intensive arable farming to keeping cattle and sheep. The land enclosures from that period can still be seen in the field systems on the island today.

The huge copper ore deposits on Parys Mountain near Amlwch had already been exploited by the Romans and, from the mid-18th century, large-scale mining was started to meet the increased demand for the metal. By 1780 the mine at Parys Mountain, owned by the industrialist Thomas Williams, was producing much of the world's copper ore. The ore was transported the short distance to Amlwch Harbour and taken by ship to copper smelters in South Wales and Lancashire. At its peak the mine employed 1,500 people, but reduced demand in the 19th century brought about a rapid decline. Today, both the enormous opencast mine at Parys Mountain and the old harbour at Amlwch are visible reminders of Anglesey's industrial past.

For thousands of years, the journey to Anglesey through the mountains of Snowdonia and across the hazardous Menai Strait, was often slow and dangerous. When Holyhead, on neighbouring Holy Island to the west of

Above *Northeast of Beaumaris is Penmon, where St Seiriol founded a monastery in the 6th century. Sacked by the Vikings in the 10th century, the monastery was rebuilt by Augustian monks during the 13th century. The ruins of their sleeping quarters and dining hall (above) adjoin St Seiriol's church which houses the intricately carved Penmon Cross.*

Below *Just a short distance across the water from Trywn Du lighthouse is little Puffin Island. Once known as Priestholm Island, it is now privately owned and designated a Special Protection Area. The public are not allowed to land on the island but several boats operate from Beaumaris to view its large seabird colonies, including that of the great cormorant.*

PUFFIN ISLAND

Puffin Island is an uninhabited island located a short distance from the northeast tip of Anglesey near Penmon. A monastery was founded on the island by St Seiriol during the 6th century and it is believed that he is buried there. Ruins of monastic buildings and a 12th century church still survive in the centre of this little island. Known by the Vikings as Priestholm, Puffin Island is now uninhabited and privately owned and visitors are not allowed to land without permission of the owners. Due to its large seabird colonies, the island has now been designated a Special Protection Area. During the late 19th century, the island's puffin population was destroyed by an influx of brown rats. In recent years efforts have been made to eradicate the rats to encourage the puffins to return.

Above *Once the worlds leading producer of copper ore, this great opencast pit at Parys Mountain, near Amlwch, is now an Industrial Heritage Trail. This dramatic and strange orange-coloured landscape has been used in more recent years as the location for films such as Dr Who.*

Below *There are now three wind farms on Anglesey, supplying electricity to the National Grid. In the centre of the island, the 34 turbines of the Llyn Alaw wind farm, completed in 1997, saves about 50,000 tonnes of carbon dioxide being pumped into the atmosphere each year.*

Anglesey, was chosen as the premier port for traffic to Ireland in the early 19th century (see pages 134-135), the engineer Thomas Telford was commissioned to improve road communications between London and Holyhead. The new route (now the A5) was finally completed in 1826 by the opening of the Menai Bridge across the Menai Strait from North Wales to Anglesey.

The opening of the Chester & Holyhead Railway in 1848 further improved communications with Anglesey. To carry trains across the Menai Strait, a new wrought-iron tubular bridge was built by the railway's engineer, Robert Stephenson. Opened in 1850, the Britannia Bridge was extensively damaged by fire in 1970. It has since been rebuilt on two levels, the upper one carrying a road and the lower one the railway.

Today, with almost its

entire coastline designated an Area of Outstanding Natural Beauty, its many beautiful sandy beaches and a multitude of historic sites, Anglesey has become dependent on tourism as its main source of economic activity. Farming, too, is still important and the island's lush, green interior supports a thriving dairy industry. There is little heavy industry on Anglesey, the one exception being the Wylfa nuclear power station which dominates the skyline around Wylfa Head on the north coast. Sadly, much of the northern and eastern interior is dominated by enormous electricity pylons that stride across the island from Wylfa to the North Wales mainland. However, as a contrast and a source of renewable energy, several wind farms have also been recently built in the centre of the island.

NATURAL HISTORY
Most of Anglesey's 100-mile long coastline is designated an Area of Outstanding Natural Beauty and includes

several protected wetland sites and nature reserves. The island's mainly agricultural interior contains several lakes, including the Llyn Alaw reservoir and Cefni Reservoir, which provide bird sanctuaries for aquatic birds.

Separating Anglesey from the mainland, the hazardous and narrow 15-mile long Menai Strait is home to a wide range of marine life, including many species of algae, sponge, sea anemone, mollusc, mussel and lobster, and a wide variety of fish including cod, bass and plaice. Located on the banks of the Menai Strait near Brynsiencyn and overlooking Caernarfon, the Anglesey Sea Zoo contains an exhibition of living sealife from around the coast of Anglesey. For more details visit their website: www.angleseyseazoo.co.uk

On the low-lying south

Above *During the late 18th century, the mine on Parys Mountain was the world's leading supplier of copper ore. The ore was conveyed the short distance to Amlwch Harbour (above) where it was either smelted or shipped to smelters in South Wales and Lancashire. At the peak of copper ore production in 1780, the village of Amlwch was said to contain over 1,000 alehouses!*

coast of the island, there are many varied habitats ranging from salt marshes and mud flats to beaches and dunes. Now a National Nature Reserve at the southern tip of Anglesey, Newborough Warren was once an area of rich farmland until huge storms in the 14th century buried the whole area in sand dunes. Once populated by hundreds of thousands of rabbits, this enormous area has been stabilized over the centuries by marram grass and now supports a wide range of important plant and bird life. To the west of the sand dunes are the pinewoods of Newborough Forest. It is the largest area of woodland on Anglesey and is one of the most important conservation sites for red squirrels in the UK.

Immediately to the west of Newborough Forest are Malltraeth Sands and the estuary of the Afon Cefni.

During the early 19th century, much of the river's meandering course from Llangefni to the sea was realigned, a sea embankment built at Malltraeth and land reclaimed for agriculture. Ditches, pools, reedbeds and marshland formed from the river's original course are now home to a wide range of rare plant and bird life and, as such, are protected as Sites of Special Scientific Interest. Charles Tunnicliffe, the internationally famous painter of birds, lived and worked in a cottage close to the Afon Cefni from 1947 until his death in 1979. Much of his work can be seen today at the Anglesey Gallery near Llangefni.

Moving to the northwest coast of Anglesey, the enormous expanse of Red Wharf Bay – at low tide its area of exposed sand and mud flats covers ten square miles – attracts large numbers of wading birds and waterfowl.

HOW TO GET THERE
By rail Stations at Llanfairpwll, Bodorgan, Ty Croes, Rhosneigr and Valley are served by local trains from Crewe, Chester, Llandudno Junction, Bangor and Holyhead.

By road The major road crossing into Anglesey is by the A55 trunk road across the Britannia Bridge from North Wales. Alternatively, there is a crossing over the narrow Menai Bridge from Bangor.

ORDNANCE SURVEY MAPS
Landranger 1:50,000 series No. 114

TOURIST INFORMATION
Llanfairpwll Tourist Information Centre, Station Site, Isle of Anglesey Gwynedd, Wales LL61 5UJ (tel. 01248 713177).

WHERE TO STAY
There is a wide range of accommodation on the Isle of Anglesey. For details contact the Tourist Information Centre at Llanfairpwll (see above) or visit the website: www.nwt.co.uk

ISLAND WALKS
The best way to see the island is on the 125-mile Anglesey Coastal Path which starts and finishes at St Cybi's Church in Holyhead on nearby Holy Island. In the south of the island, Newborough Forest is crisscrossed with a series of forest trails.

There are also 14 way-marked circular walks that follow the trail of Celtic saints. For more details contact Llanfairpwll Tourist Information Centre (see above).

PLACES TO VISIT
- Beaumaris Castle
- Wylfa visitor centre
- Amlwch Harbour
- Parys Mountain copper mine
- Plas Newydd (NT)
- St Seiriol's church and priory at Penmon
- Lligwy burial chamber
- Din Lligwy Romano-Celtic settlement
- Bryn Celli Ddu burial chamber
- Barclodiad y Gawres burial chamber

Right *Designed by Thomas Telford as an important link in the London to Holyhead mail route, the graceful Menai Suspension Bridge became the first physical connection between Anglesey and the mainland when it was completed in 1826.*

Below *The Britannia Tubular Bridge was designed by Roberet Stephenson to carry the Chester to Holyhead railway. It opened in 1850 but was damaged by fire in 1970. The bridge has since been rebuilt to carry road and railway traffic on two separate levels.*

THE LONGEST PLACE NAME

A village on the Isle of Anglesey has the longest place name in the UK. Usually abbreviated to Llanfair PG or Llanfairpwll, the full spelling of the 58 characters is as follows: Llanfairpwllgwyngyllgogerychwyrndrobwllllantysiliogogogoch. Translated this means 'St Mary's church in the hollow of the white hazel near to the rapid whirlpool and the church of St Tysilio of the red cave'. Located on the Bangor to Holyhead railway line, the railway station at Llanfairpwll was closed in 1966 but reopened in 1974. With its world-famous name board the station has now become a tourist attraction in itself. The full name is also registered as the longest single word '.com' domain in the world.

HOLY ISLAND

Holyhead Bay

North Stack

ANGLESEY

Holyhead Mountain

Holyhead

South Stack Lighthouse

A55 Coastal Park

A5025

B4545

Trearddur

Valley

HOLY ISLAND

0   kilometres   10
0   miles   6

Along with neighbouring Anglesey, Holy Island was one of the last strongholds of the ancient Celts in Britain until they were savagely defeated by the Romans in 78AD. Following a period as a lonely Roman military outpost, in the 6th century Holy Island became a centre for early Christian monks led by St Cybi. During the 19th century, improved communications from the mainland ensured that Holyhead became the premier port for the fast-growing and lucrative traffic across the Irish Sea to Ireland - a position it still holds today.

HISTORY

Inevitably, the history of Holy Island is closely linked with that of neighbouring Anglesey (see pages 126-133). Both islands have been occupied since the Middle Stone Age and remains from the later Neolithic period, such as standing stones and a chambered long barrow, can be seen on Holy Island. Later, both islands became a stronghold for an ancient Celtic tribe known as the Ordovices. Remains from this period, such as the Iron Age hillfort on Holyhead Mountain, can be seen by visitors to Holy Island today.

Following their invasion of Britain in 43AD, the Romans swiftly moved to subdue the rebellious Celtic tribes throughout the land. Anglesey and Holy Island became one of the last Celtic strongholds, but the Druidic Celts were finally crushingly defeated on Anglesey by a Roman army led by Agricola in 78AD. Holy Island then became one of the loneliest military outposts in the Roman Empire and, to guard against attack by Irish pirates, a signal tower was built on top of Holyhead Mountain. The Romans also built an unusual three-walled fort around the harbour where St Cybi's Church in Holyhead now stands.

After the Romans left, Holy Island, along with Anglesey, was occupied by a succession of invaders, from Irish pirates and Saxons to Vikings and Normans, until it fell to the English king, Edward I, in the 13th century.

Above *After the opening of the Chester & Holyhead Railway in 1848, Holyhead not only became the premier port for passenger and freight traffic to Ireland, but also for the prestigious Irish Mail service. Holyhead's present railway station was greatly enlarged by the London & North Western Railway in 1880.*

Below *One of the world's largest ferry operators, Stena Line, operates the ferry service between Ireland and Holyhead. Here, the 44,000-ton* Stena Adventurer, *built by Hyundai Heavy Industries in South Korea in 2003, approaches Holyhead from Dublin as two kayaks set off from Porth Namarch on their journey around Holy Island's Heritage Coast.*

From the time of the ancient Celts, religion had always played an important role on Holy Island. In 540AD, St Cybi founded a monastery within the grounds of the abandoned Roman fort in Holyhead. The original monastery was sacked by the Vikings in the 10th century but later rebuilt in the 13th century.

Although for thousands of years Holyhead was the nearest port to Ireland, the journey from England through Snowdonia and across the Menai Strait was often slow and dangerous. This all changed in 1801, when the United Kingdom of Great Britain & Ireland was created. To improve links with Ireland, Thomas Telford built a post road from London to Holyhead (now known as the A5). A causeway was also built to link Holy Island with Anglesey. The route was finally completed in 1826 by the opening of the Menai Bridge across the Menai Strait from North Wales to Anglesey.

The opening of the Chester & Holyhead Railway in 1848 further strengthened the town's position as the premier port for Ireland. During the last half of the 19th century, major improvements were also made to the harbour, including the building of a massive breakwater, warehouses, hotels, and an improved railway infrastructure. For a short period between 1909 and 1910, transatlantic liners on the Liverpool to New York route also stopped off at Holyhead.

Today the town of Holyhead, still an important port for traffic across the Irish Sea, is also home to an enormous aluminium smelter which provides important employment on the island. Holyhead apart, much of the rest of Holy Island is now designated as an Area of Outstanding Natural Beauty and includes a section of Heritage Coast.

NATURAL HISTORY

The Holyhead Mountain Heritage Coast runs for eight miles from North Stack, in the north of the island, to the sandy beaches of Trearddur Bay on the west coast. It includes the spectacular cliffs around South Stack that attract thousands of nesting seabirds every year. The RSPB have set up a birdwatching station at Ellins Tower near South Stack, where birdwatchers can observe the large colonies of guillemot, razorbill and kittiwake. Also to be seen here during the breeding season are a small colony of puffin, peregrine falcon, and a few pairs of the rare chough.

Holy Island's rugged northwest coastline is also a Special Area of Conservation. In addition to its carpet of heather, the cliff heathland supports many maritime wildflowers, from sea campion and thrift to bird-foot trefoil and the rare spotted rock rose.

HOW TO GET THERE

By road The A5 trunk road terminates at Holyhead. The B4545 crosses Four Mile Bridge between the village of Valley on Anglesey to the southern part of Holy Island.

By rail Regular train services operate to Holyhead from Anglesey, North Wales and England including a direct service from London.

By sea Stena Line operates a regular ferry service to Holyhead from Dublin and Dun Laoghaire in Ireland.

ORDNANCE SURVEY MAPS

Landranger 1:50,000 series No. 114

TOURIST INFORMATION

Holyhead Tourist Information Centre, Stena Line Terminal 1, Holyhead, Isle of Anglesey LL65 1DQ (tel. 01407 762 622).

WHERE TO STAY

There is a wide range of accommodation available on Holy Island, especially in Holyhead. For more details contact Holyhead Tourist Information Centre (see above) or visit the official tourist website for the region: www.nwt.co.uk

Above *South Stack lighthouse was built in 1809 to warn shipping of the treacherous rocks around the north coast of Holy Island. Following restoration, the lighthouse is now open to the public - access is via 400 steps!*

ISLAND WALKS

In the north of the island there are footpaths around Holyhead Mountain, with its Iron Age hillfort, prehistoric hut circles and fine views across the Irish Sea and to Snowdonia. The 125-mile Anglesey Coastal Path starts and finishes at St Cybi's Church in Holyhead. Set in a disused quarry near Holyhead, the Holyhead Breakwater Country Park contains a series of nature trails.

PLACES TO VISIT

● Ellin's Tower Seabird Centre at South Stack (RSPB)
● South Stack lighthouse
● Holyhead Breakwater Country Park
● St Cybi's Church and remains of three-walled Roman fort in Holyhead
● Iron Age hillfort, Roman signal station and prehistoric hut circles on Holyhead Mountain

BARDSEY ISLAND

St George's Channel

Aberdaron

LLYEN PENINSULA

Bardsey Sound

St Mary's Abbey (rems)

Mynydd Enlli

BARDSEY ISLAND

Jetty

Lighthouse

| 0 | kilometres | 5 |
| 0 | miles | 3 |

Since the founding of an early Christian monastery in the 6th century by St Cadfan, Bardsey Island has been a centre for religious pilgrimage. For centuries, farming has also been important to island life and major improvements for its tenants were carried out in 1870 by the island's wealthy owner, Lord Newborough. Owned by the Bardsey Island Trust since 1979 the island, with its internationally important wildlife, is now a National Nature Reserve, a Site of Special Scientific Interest and an Area of Outstanding Natural Beauty.

HISTORY

Archæological remains show that Bardsey Island has been occupied for several thousand years. During the 6th century, early Christians were attracted to the island's solitude for prayer and meditation. St Cadfan (c.530AD–c.590AD), a nobleman from Brittany, established a monastery on Bardsey during this period and it is thought that he and many of his followers (and supposedly 20,000 saints!) are buried in the Abbey's graveyard. The present ruins are those of the Augustinian Abbey of St Mary's, which was built during the 13th century and continued in use until the Dissolution of the Monasteries during the reign of Henry VIII. The discovery of the remains of medieval agricultural buildings in the north of the island also show that farming on Bardsey has always been important and this practice continues to the present day.

During the 19th century, Bardsey came under the ownership of a wealthy Victorian landowner, Lord Newborough. Most of the sturdy stone houses that can be seen on Bardsey today were built in the 1870s to provide improved accommodation for his tenants. The island continued to be owned and farmed by successive generations of the Newborough family but in 1925, most of the islanders left for an easier life on the mainland. In 1972 the island was sold to Lord Cowdray, one of the wealthiest men in Britain. Finally, in 1979, the Bardsey Island Trust was able to purchase the

Below *The 548ft-high Mynydd Enlli towers over the fields and bays of Bardsey. Its eastern cliff are home to a wide variety of sea birds while the rocky bays, such as Henllwyn (below) are rich in marine life. Here, visitors to the island can regularly see large numbers of Atlantic grey seal basking on the rocks. To the south of the bay, across a narrow isthmus, is the unusual square-sided lighthouse which was built in 1821.*

Above *At the northern end of Bardsey are the 13th century remains of the Abbey of St Mary's. Nestling close to an old farm and more recent, 19th century, houses, the graveyard is said to contain the remains of St Cadfan and 20,000 other saints.*

island and, to protect its rich and rare variety of wildlife, it has since become a National Nature Reserve and a Site of Special Scientific Interest.

NATURAL HISTORY

Apart from the steep slopes of Mynydd Enlli, the remainder of the island is fairly flat and low-lying. Here, a network of

fields and stone walls bear testimony to the many centuries of farming on Bardsey. The island and the surrounding seas are internationally important for their wildlife and, in order to protect this fragile ecosystem, the Bardsey Island Trust works closely with many other conservation bodies.

Many rare plants grow on the island,

including over 300 species of lichen. The Bardsey Apple is said to grow on the world's rarest apple tree.

Between the spring and autumn, Bardsey is an important breeding ground for migratory birds. Nearly 100 different species are sometimes counted on the island, including many types of warbler and an enormous colony of nocturnal Manx shearwater. Other species such as raven, chough and oysercatcher regularly nest on the island. Seabirds, such as razorbill, guillemot, shag and kittiwake breed along the steep eastern cliffs of Mynydd Enlli.

Below *Seen from the slopes of Mynydd Enlli, a centuries-old pattern of fields covers the low-lying western half of Bardsey. Most of the houses on the island were built by Lord Newbourough in the 1870s.*

Close inshore, the inlets and bays are visited by Atlantic grey seal, which visitors can often see basking in large numbers on the rocks. Porpoise and dolphin are also regular visitors to the seas around Bardsey.

How to Get There
Bardsey Island lies two miles across Bardsey Sound from the southwest point of the Lleyn Peninsula. Daytrips are run by the Bardsey Island ferry and normally leave from Porth Meudwy, near Aberdaron, or from Pwllheli. For details contact the ferry office in Pwllheli (tel. 08458 1136554) or visit the Bardsey Island Trust's website: www.bardsey.org No dogs are allowed on the island.

Ordnance Survey Maps
Landranger 1:50,000 series No. 123

Tourist Information
Pwllheli Tourist Information Centre, Min y Don, Sgwar yr Orsaf, Pwllheli LL53 5HG (tel. 01758 613000). There is also an information point in Abersoch (tel. 01758 712929) or visit www.gwynedd.gov.uk

Where to Stay
The Bardsey Island Trust has a number of self-catering properties on the island. Accommodation is also available at the Bird and Field Observatory. For details contact the Trust's office (tel. 08458 112233) or visit their website: www.bardsey.org

For accommodation on the mainland contact the Tourist Information Centres in Abersoch (tel. 01758 712929) or Pwllheli (tel. 01758 613000).

Camping is not allowed on the island.

ISLAND WALKS

Apart from a few tractors and electric buggies, Bardsey Island is traffic-free. In addition to the central track that runs from the lighthouse in the south to the Abbey ruins in the north, there is a marked footpath that follows the west coast of the island. A steep footpath also leads to the summit of Mynydd Enlli where there are good views of the Lleyn Peninsula.

PLACES TO VISIT

● Ruins of St Mary's Abbey
● Bird and Field Observatory

Right *For centuries, farming has been important on Bardsey. As a National Nature Reserve, great care is taken to protect the fragile flora and fauna. Sheep are grazed on the island to help preserve wildlife habitats.*

RAMSEY ISLAND

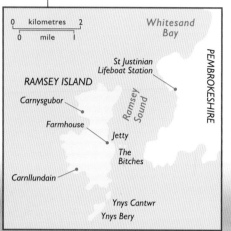

Separated from the Pembrokeshire mainland by the dangerous currents of Ramsey Sound, Ramsey Island was intensively farmed from Bronze Age times until the end of the 20th century. From the 6th century, it also became a centre for early Christian monks, with their headquarters in nearby St David's and, from the 11th century, an important destination for pilgrims. Owned by the Church for over 1,200 years, Ramsey is now owned and managed as a National Nature Reserve by the Royal Society for the Protection of Birds.

Below *Overlooking the island's small jetty and the turbulent waters of Ramsey Sound, the farmhouse is the only substantial building on the island and home to an RSPB warden. The two small rocks in the channel are known as Bitches and Whelps.*

HISTORY

Archaeological remains in the shape of cairns and field systems found on Ramsey Island show that it has been inhabited and farmed since the Bronze Age. The cairns are found on the summits of Carn Ysgubor and Carn Llundain. During the 6th century, early Christians including St David, the patron saint of Wales, founded a monastic order in the nearby mainland tiny city that now carries his name. Ramsey Island became part of the lands that were owned and administered by the Bishops of St David's and a chapel was built on the island. Ramsey not only became a

retreat for the monks of St David's but also, from the 11th century onwards, increasingly important as a place of pilgrimage for Christians.

From as far back as the Bronze Age, farming had also been an important activity on Ramsey. This continued under the Church's ownership and, after 1905, under private ownership. The island's fertile soil supported mixed farming including the raising of beef cattle, goats and sheep. Crops such as barley, oats and wheat and vegetables were also grown. Up to the early 20th century a lime kiln and corn mill were also in use on Ramsey. In addition to

farming, the islanders also supplemented their income by collecting gull, puffin and guillemot eggs.

Towards the end of the 20th century, there was also a commercial deer farm on the island. When this enterprise closed down, the remaining deer were left on the island and can be seen by visitors today. In more recent years, Ramsey Island has been owned and managed by the Royal Society for the Protection of Birds (RSPB) and is now a designated Site of Special Scientific Interest, a National Nature Reserve, a Special Protection Area and a Special Area of Conservation.

NATURAL HISTORY

As an important site for a wide range of wildlife, Ramsey is now owned and managed by the RSPB. A resident warden lives on the island. The area of grassland in the northern part of the island, grazed by rabbits and sheep, is an ideal feeding ground for chough, which nest in caves along the rugged coastline during springtime. At this time of the year, when the slopes are covered in an array of colourful flowers, keen-eyed visitors can also see peregrines and ravens

Above *Close to Ramsey Island's rugged south coast, and included within the boundary of the National Nature Reserve, are the small islands of Ynys Cantwr and Ynys Bery.*

nesting on the cliffs. Ramsey is also an important stopping off point for migrant birds between spring and autumn, including wheatear, which make their nests in the miles of old drystone boundary walls that criss-cross the island.

During the summer months, the rocky ledges around the coast are home to colonies of seabirds including razorbill, guillemot, fulmar and kittiwake. During late summer, the area of heathland in the south east of Ramsey Island, home to

GOLDEN HAIR LICHEN

Found on the western slopes of Carn Llundain on Ramsey Island, the rare golden hair lichen is one of the most pollution-sensitive lichens in the UK. Due to increases in atmospheric pollution during the last 100 years, the golden hair has dramatically declined and is now only found at a few sites in southwest England and Anglesey, as well as on Ramsey. The golden hair lichen or *Teloschistes flavicans*, is protected by law and is listed as world-wide threatened and declining species.

lapwing and many heathland plants, is ablaze with colour.

Autumn is the time to see the largest colony of Atlantic grey seal in southern Britain, with their newly-born pups on the beaches and in the coves around Ramsey's dramatic coastline.

HOW TO GET THERE

Between April and October, boats operate from St Justinian's lifeboat station, two miles west of St David's, to Ramsey Island. Visitor numbers are limited. Due to a shortage of suitable car parking space at St Justinian, it is recommended that visitors to Ramsey Island make use of the hourly shuttle bus from St David's to St Justinian between April and September. For further details contact Thousand Island Expeditions, Cross Square, St David's, Pembrokeshire SA62 6SL (tel. 01437 721686 or 01437 721721) or visit their website: www.thousandislands.co.uk No dogs are allowed on the island.

Below *Nearly 200ft high, the crumbling cliffs overlooking Aber Mawr on Ramsey's west coast are constantly being eroded by the wind and sea and burrowing rabbits. The cliffs are unfenced and visitors are urged to take caution. In the distance can be seen the 500ft high craggy peaks of Carn Hen and Carn-ffald near St David's Head on the mainland.*

ORDNANCE SURVEY MAPS
Landranger 1:50,000 series No. 157

TOURIST INFORMATION
St David's Tourist Information Centre
(independent TIC), The Grove,
St David's, Pembrokeshire
(tel: 01437 720392).

WHERE TO STAY
There are limited facilities and no
accommodation is available to the public
on Ramsey Island. Camping is not
allowed on the island. A wide variety of
accommodation from camp sites and
caravan parks to self-catering and hotels
is available on the nearby mainland
around St David's. For further details,
either contact St David's Tourist
Information Centre (see above) or visit
the official tourist information website:
www.visitpembrokeshire.com

ISLAND WALKS
A circular footpath of just over three
miles in length starts and finishes at the
farmhouse on Ramsey Island. No dogs
are allowed on the island.

PLACES TO VISIT
● RSPB information centre and shop
● The summits of Carn Ysgubor and
Carn Llundain
● Site of rare golden hair on western
slopes of Carn Llundain

Right *Between April and October a regular
boat service leaves St Justinian lifeboat station
for the short but sometimes turbulent crossing
to Ramsey Island, seen in the distance*

SKOMER ISLAND

SKOMER ISLAND

The Wick

The Neck

MIDLAND ISLE Martin's Haven

PEMBROKESHIRE

Marine Nature Reserve

Information Centre

Broad Sound

GATEHOLM ISLAND

Lighthouse

SKOKHOLM ISLAND

0 kilometres 2
0 mile 1

L ying a mile off the coast of Pembrokeshire, Skomer Island was occupied by farmers from the Iron Age to the mid-20th century. Once also a thriving commercial rabbit warrenry, the island has now become an internationally important centre for the study of migrating seabirds. In particular, Skomer is famous for its enormous colonies of puffins and Manx shearwaters, which descend on the island during the breeding season. Skomer is a National Nature Reserve and a Site of Special Scientific Interest, while the seas around it are a Marine Nature Reserve.

HISTORY

Skomer has been occupied by man for over 2,000 years, and the island is covered with remains of settlements, field systems and cairns from the entire period. Because of its archaeological importance, most of Skomer is now a scheduled Ancient Monument. A modern field system has been in place in the centre of the island for over 1,000 years and, until 1950, this managed to support a farmer and his family. The present farmhouse, now being renovated, dates from the early 19th century. The Vikings certainly visited the region in the 10th century, and all of the islands off the Pembrokeshire coast carry names that reflect the Norsemen's influence.

In the 13th century, a rabbit warren was established on Skomer, and the fur and meat provided a valuable income for the island until the arrival of myxomatosis after World War II. Over the centuries, Skomer has had many owners including the 5th Lord Kensington, who purchased the island in 1897. During the early 20th century, Skomer was leased to J. J. Neale, an eminent Welsh naturalist, who turned the island into a wildlife sanctuary. The last residents and farmer left the island for good in 1950 and, in 1958, the island was purchased as a nature reserve jointly by the West Wales Field Society and the Nature Conservancy. In 1959 Skomer was declared a National Nature Reserve and, later, a Site of Special Scientific Interest and a Special Protection Area. It

Below *During June, swathes of red campion carpet the island of Skomer. In the distance is The Neck - a small extension of Skomer linked to the island by a narrow isthmus. The strong currents of the narrow channel that separates Skomer from the mainland, Jack Sound, are a dangerous spot for boatmen.*

is now managed by the Wildlife Trust of South and West Wales for the owners, the Countryside Council for Wales. The sea around Skomer, known as the Pembrokeshire Marine Special Area of Conservation, is a European Marine Site.

NATURAL HISTORY

A naturalist's paradise, Skomer is internationally famous as a breeding ground for vast numbers of seabirds. Most famous are the 6,000 pairs of puffin that breed in burrows on the island from late March until August. Visitors to the island during this period can experience these wonderful characters at very close quarters. More difficult to see, due to their nocturnal habits, are the 150,000 pairs of Manx shearwaters who return to their same burrows on Skomer year after year, following their 6,000 mile flight from the coast of South America. The storm petrel, also a nocturnal creature, is also found on Skomer but in much smaller numbers.

The dramatic cliffs around Skomer are also home to many thousands of seabirds, including razorbill, guillemot, kittiwake and fulmar. During the nesting season, the coastline of Skomer resembles the seabird equivalent of a city rush hour. Thousands of gulls, from the small kittiwake to the great black-backed gull, add to the din!

Skomer is also visited by many other migratory birds, such as finch, swallow, warbler and pipit. Resident birds

Above *During June, the air and ground around The Wick is thick with puffins returning to their burrows with sand eels for their young. These delightful seabirds seem to have no fear of humans.*

Above *Skomer is an important breeding ground for thousands of guillemots and razorbills. During the breeding season, the cliffs and ledges around the island witness a constant flow of these birds going about their business. The single chicks hatch in early June and by early August they have left their nests.*

on this tree-less island also include blackbird, dunnock, wren, pheasant, wood pigeon, magpie and carrion crow. No wonder that Skomer is a mecca for birdwatchers!

In addition to its teeming birdlife, Skomer is still inhabited by the descendants of the 14th century rabbit warren. Some have even bred with more exotic, domesticated breeds, producing some interesting results. Their extensive burrows also provide home to the visiting Manx shearwater. Other mammals found on Skomer include the Skomer vole and wood mouse. Both of these and also the rabbits provide food for marauding gulls.

Rich in marine life, the seas around Skomer are now a designated European Marine Site. During the late summer period, grey seals breed in the rocky coves and bays around the island, while dolphins and porpoises can regularly be seen offshore.

In addition to its teeming birdlife, Skomer is rich in plant life. In late spring, this tree-less island is covered in bluebells and, by early summer, swathes of red campion provide a stunning backdrop to the wheeling and diving seabirds. The cliffs support many plants, from sea campion to sea mayweed, while the ancient field system and boundary walls in the centre of Skomer provide shelter for wood sage and foxglove. Giving scientists a guide to the state of our environment, many rare species of pollution-sensitive lichen can also be seen on the old field walls and rock faces.

HOW TO GET THERE
Between April and October, a regular boat service operates in the mornings (except Mondays) from Martin's Haven (near Marloes) to land on Skomer. There are limits on the numbers allowed to land on the island. Advance booking is not possible. There are also cruises around Skomer and the island of Grassholm from Martin's Haven. For more information contact Dale Sailing (tel. 01646 603123/603110) or visit their website: www.dale-sailing.co.uk Dogs are not allowed on the island.

ORDNANCE SURVEY MAPS
Landranger 1:50,000 series No. 157

TOURIST INFORMATION
Nearest tourist information centre on the mainland is at Milford Haven. Milford Haven Tourist Information Centre, 94 Charles Street, Milford Haven, Pembrokeshire SA73 2HL (tel. 01646 690866) or visit their website: www.pembrokeshire.gov.uk

WHERE TO STAY
There is no accommodation available for visitors on Skomer, although an extensive building programme at the

farm is currently underway. For further details contact The Welsh Wildlife Centre (tel. 01239 621212). Camping is not allowed on the island.

There is a wide range of accommodation available on the mainland, ranging from camp sites and caravan parks to self-catering and hotels. For further details contact the Milford Haven Tourist Information Centre (see above).

ISLAND WALKS

Skomer is traffic-free and there is an extensive network of footpaths around the island. The Wildlife Trust of South and West Wales publish a detailed guide of the island which clearly shows where it is possible to walk. Walkers are requested to keep to the footpaths to avoid damaging the thousands of puffin and Manx shearwater burrows. On Skomer, puffins have the right of way!

Above *On the south side of Skomer, the steep-sided inlet known as The Wick is a favourite spot for birdwatchers. Thousands of seabirds, including razorbill, guillemot, kittiwake and fulmar, nest on the cliffs. The clifftop at the head of the inlet is one of the best places on Skomer to see puffin.*

Below *To the south of Skomer lies the island of Skokholm. This 247-acre island was purchased by the Welsh Wildlife Trusts in 2006.*

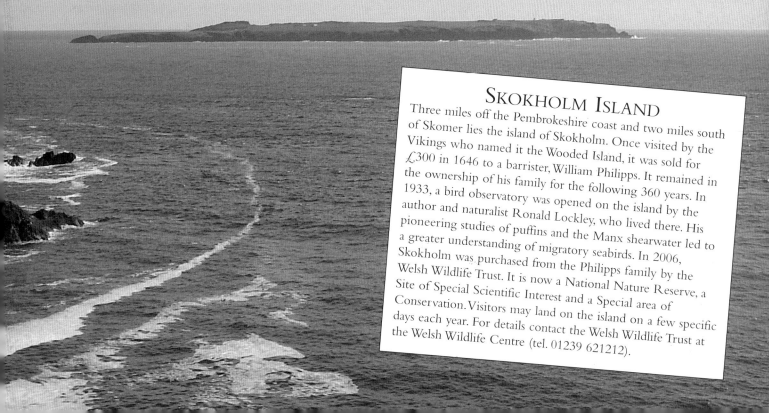

SKOKHOLM ISLAND

Three miles off the Pembrokeshire coast and two miles south of Skomer lies the island of Skokholm. Once visited by the Vikings who named it the Wooded Island, it was sold for £300 in 1646 to a barrister, William Philipps. It remained in the ownership of his family for the following 360 years. In 1933, a bird observatory was opened on the island by the author and naturalist Ronald Lockley, who lived there. His pioneering studies of puffins and the Manx shearwater led to a greater understanding of migratory seabirds. In 2006, Skokholm was purchased from the Philipps family by the Welsh Wildlife Trust. It is now a National Nature Reserve, a Site of Special Scientific Interest and a Special area of Conservation. Visitors may land on the island on a few specific days each year. For details contact the Welsh Wildlife Trust at the Welsh Wildlife Centre (tel. 01239 621212).

CALDEY ISLAND

Inhabited since the Stone Age, Caldey Island became a place of worship for Celtic Christians in the 6th century. Apart from Viking raids and ownership by a Norman nobleman, the Old Priory remained in use until 1536. Over the following centuries, Caldey had many owners until Benedictine monks settled there in 1899. The present Abbey was completed in 1913, but near bankruptcy forced them to sell Caldey to the present order of Cistercian monks. The island is now a self-sufficient and thriving religious community that attracts visitors in their thousands.

Tenby

PEMBROKESHIRE

ST CATHERINE'S ISLAND

Carmarthen Bay

Penally

0   kilometres   2
0   mile   1

ST MARGARET'S ISLAND

Priory Bay

Jetty

Monastery

Sandtop Bay

Priory

CALDEY ISLAND

Chapel Point

Lighthouse

Below *Close to the landing jetty on the north coast of Caldey, the uncrowded and clean, sandy Priory Beach offers peace, seclusion and safe bathing. From here there are good views across to the Pembrokeshire coast and the popular seaside resort of Tenby.*

HISTORY

Archæologists have discovered human bones and flint tools in Nanna's Cave on Caldey, which show that the island has been inhabited since the Middle Stone Age – over 10,000 years ago. At that time, Caldey was still joined to the mainland and the coast would have been some distance away. These hunters and gatherers had evolved into the first farmers by about 3500BC.

Early Celtic Christians, led by a hermit called Pyro, first came to Caldey in the 6th century and established a small chapel on the island. Others followed and settled in a small community round the chapel. By the 10th century, however, Viking raiders had probably forced the Christians to flee. The island derives its name from the Norse 'Cold Island'.

In 1131, Caldey was given to a Norman nobleman by Henry I, and it was later given to the Benedictine monks of St Dogmael's. The monks built a priory on the island, and this remained in use until the Dissolution of the Monasteries in 1536, when Caldey was given by Henry VIII to John Bradshawe of Presteign. Over the following centuries, the island had many owners who farmed on the island, until it was bought by a master and chaplain of Harrow School, Rev W D Bushell, in 1897.

Bushell set to restoring the old priory and two churches and, in 1899, invited a

small group of Benedictine monks, led by Benjamin Carlyle, to re-establish the monastery on Caldey. Bushell sold it to them in 1906. The present impressive, Italian-style abbey, was built and completed in 1913, but its enormous cost forced the monks to sell Caldey to the Reformed Cistercian Order of monks in 1925. The Benedictine monks stayed on until 1928, when they moved to more modest surroundings at Prinknash in Gloucestershire.

The following year, Cistercian monks from Scourmont Abbey in Belgium moved in to Caldey. Since then, despite early problems with day-trippers, the monks have developed Caldey into a self-sufficient island home. Much of their income is derived from a thriving perfume industry, and the thousands of day-trippers who visit Caldey every year.

The lighthouse on Caldey was erected in 1829 and was automated in 1927. It was the last Trinity House lighthouse to be powered by acetylene gas, and was not electrified until as recently as 1997.

Above *Caldey's Cistercian Abbey, with its whitewashed walls and terracotta tiles, was completed in 1913. Its enormous cost nearly bankrupted the Benedictine monks who built it. Caldey Island and its abbey were sold to the present Cistercian order in 1925.*

Left *Originally built as a fortified house in the 12th century by its owner, Norman nobleman Robert Fitzmartin, the Old Priory was further extended by Benedictine monks when they came to live on Caldey. Above the archway into the courtyard, the old building is now occupied by a family of white doves.*

mixture of acid and alkaline soils, a colourful carpet of wild flowers covers Caldey during the summer months. Seabirds, including auk and large numbers of gull, breed along the clifftops around Red Berry Bay, and chough are known to make their home in remote caves along the coastline.

HOW TO GET THERE
A regular service of passenger boats runs from Tenby Harbour to Caldey between Easter and October. The island is closed to the public on Sundays. Dogs are allowed on the island, but must be kept on the leash at all times.

ORDNANCE SURVEY MAPS
Landranger 1:50,000 series No. 158

NATURAL HISTORY
Caldey Island and the nearby nature reserve on St Margaret's Island are home to a large colony of Atlantic grey seal, and visitors to the island can often spot them basking on rocks along the island's rugged southern coastline. Dolphin and porpoise are regularly seen in the seas around Caldey.

Most of Caldey has been farmed for centuries and is home to both hedgehogs and rats. Because of these predators, ground-nesting birds do not thrive on the island. However, due to Caldey's

ST MARGARET'S ISLAND
Adjoining the west of Caldey Island at low tide is little St Margaret's Island. A chapel once stood here but in the 19th century the island was quarried for limestone. It is now a nature reserve due to the large number of seabirds, including cormorants, razorbills, shags and guillemots, that nest along its cliffs. The public are not allowed access to the island.

TOURIST INFORMATION

Tenby Tourist Information Centre,
Unit 2, Upper Park Road,
Tenby SA70 7LT
(tel. 01834 842402/842404) or visit their
website: www.visitpembrokeshire.com

WHERE TO STAY

Accommodation is available on Caldey
Island at St Philomena's Retreat House.
For more details visit the website:
www.caldey-island.co.uk

There is also a privately owned house
on the island offering self-catering
accommodation. For more details visit
the website: www.visitcaldey.co.uk

Around Tenby, there is a wide range of
accommodation ranging from campsites
and caravan parks to self-catering and
hotels. For more details contact the Tenby
Tourist Information Centre (see above).
Camping is not allowed on the island.

ISLAND WALKS

Apart from a few farm tractors, a couple
of old cars, the island fire engine and
some electric buggies, Caldey is traffic-
free. A series of signposted tracks and
footpaths enable the visitor to explore
the eastern half of the island. There is no
public access to the monastery enclosure.

PLACES TO VISIT

- Chapel of Our Lady of Peace
- Calvary
- St David's Church
- Abbey Church
- St Illtud's Church and Caldey Stone
- The Old Priory
- Chocolate factory

Right *Adjoining the priory in the centre of
the island is St Illtyd's church. Its leaning
tower dates from the 14th century. Inside the
church is the famous 6th century Caldey
Stone, inscribed in both Latin and Ogham.*

Below *On the south coast of Caldey,
crumbling Old Red Sandstone cliffs tower over
Red Berry Bay. The north side of the island is
made up of carboniferous limestone, and caves
here have yielded up human remains and flint
tools dating back to the Stone Age.*

FLAT HOLM

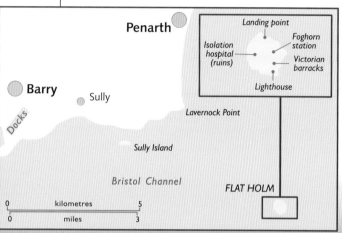

Lying just three miles from the South Wales coastline, tiny Flat Holm has a fascinating history of human occupation dating back to early Christian times. Its solitude first attracted Welsh monks who spent time in meditation on the island. Later it was probably used by the Vikings as a base from which to attack settlements around the Bristol Channel, before becoming the home of farmers and a haven for smugglers. During the 1860s, Flat Holm was turned into a heavily-armed fortress during Britain's paranoid fear over an attack from France. The attack never came and the island then became the site of an isolation hospital in the fight against the spread of cholera. During World War II, the island again became an armed fortress in the battle against the Luftwaffe. Flat Holm is now protected as a Site of Special Scientific Interest and is a Local Nature Reserve.

HISTORY

The earliest recorded occupation of Flat Holm was by the Welsh saint, Cadoc, who stayed on the island for meditation and prayer during the latter part of the 6th century. It is also recorded that Flat Holm was visited by Vikings during their raids on settlements around the Bristol Channel. After the Norman invasion, Flat Holm became the property of the Lords of Glamorgan and archæological evidence has been unearthed on the

Left During World War II, several batteries of anti-aircraft guns were established on Flat Holm to defend the nearby cities of Cardiff and Bristol from air attack. Remains of this military occupation, such as this mounting for a radar platform and false horizon, can still be seen scattered over the island.

island to show that it was occupied by farmers from about the 13th century.

By the 16th century, Flat Holm had become the property of the Earls of Bute and for several centuries was leased to tenant farmers. Also used as a rabbit warren, the island had, by the 17th century, become a haven for smugglers.

Following several serious shipwrecks and consequent loss of life in the waters around the island, a privately-funded lighthouse - a simple stone tower topped off with a coal brazier - was built in 1737. This was later considered inadequate and converted to house an oil-burning light in 1820. Trinity House took over the lighthouse in 1823 and it was converted to electric operation in 1969. Unmanned since 1988, the lighthouse now runs on solar power.

During the 1860s, when Britain feared attack from France, Flat Holm was turned into a military fortress. By 1869 four batteries, totalling nine 7-inch guns, had been installed on the island. Never used in anger, their circular pits, together with underground magazines and abandoned 7-ton cannon, can still be seen. To house the soldiers manning the batteries, a barracks was built near the lighthouse. This substantial building is used today as an education centre.

In 1884, in an effort to halt the spread of cholera from infected sailors returning from abroad, Cardiff Corporation established an isolation hospital on Flat Holm. By 1896, a permanent building had been erected and sailors suffering not only from cholera, but also plague and yellow fever, were removed from their boats to the hospital before entering port. The hospital was closed in 1935 and now lies in ruins.

An historic event occurred at the end of the 19th century, when the Italian inventor Guglielmo Marconi came to Flat Holm and successfully transmitted the world's first wireless messages over water. Marconi erected an aerial on the island and one at Lavernock Point on the Welsh coast, three miles to the northwest. On 13 May 1897, Marconi's historic message in Morse code, 'Are you ready?', was sucessfully sent and received.

Due to its strategic position in the Bristol Channel, Flat Holm was once again taken over by the military during World War II. From 1941, over 300 soldiers were based on the island, manning a range of heavy and light

Above *Erected in 1908, this fog horn station provided warning to ships in the Bristol Channel. Its enormous megaphones, powered by compressed air, could be heard over 30 miles away. Although shut down in 1988, its equipment has now been restored and is tested on special occasions.*

Below *Flat Holm, here seen from the neighbouring island of Steep Holm, is now a Site of Special Scientific Interest and a Local Nature Reserve. The island falls within the boundaries of the modern city of Cardiff which, with its famous Millennium Stadium, can be seen in the distance.*

anti-aircraft guns and a radar station in the defence of the Bristol Channel ports. A light railway was also constructed to convey provisions and ammunition from the pier at the north of the island to the various gun batteries and magazines scattered around the island.

Following a period after the war when the island was again farmed, Flat Holm was designated a Site of Special Scientific Interest in 1972 and, in 1977, became a Local Nature Reserve. Now owned by Cardiff County Council, the island is managed by the Flat Holm Project.

Below *These fenced-off ruins are all that remain of the isolation hospital built on Flat Holm in 1896. Sailors infected with cholera and other infectious diseases were taken off their boats before entering port and transferred to the island hospital.*

NATURAL HISTORY

Low-lying Flat Holm is a visible part of the carboniferous limestone that stretches under the Bristol Channel from England to South Wales. Of particular interest to geologists is the wave cut limestone platform on the beach at the west side of the island.

An important wildlife site, Flat Holm's long history of farming and military occupation has turned the island into a unique habitat for plant life. In particular, the island is one of the few places in Britain where the rare wild leek and wild peony still grow. These, and many other plants found on the island, were probably introduced over the centuries for their medicinal properties. A profusion of colour in the summer, Flat Holm

Above *Remains of a World War II searchlight housing on Flat Holm overlooks shipping in the dangerous tidal waters of the Bristol Channel. In the far distance is the English resort of Weston-super-Mare.*

is also home to many butterflies including red admiral, peacock and common blue. Under the auspices of the Flat Holm Project, scrubland in the northern part of the island has recently been cleared and restored to grassland with help of sheep.

Flat Holm is also home to about 4,000 pairs of lesser black backed gull - the largest colony in Wales - and, during the nesting season, visitors are recommended to wear hats to protect them from flying guano! A smaller number of herring gull and shelduck also nest on the island which is also visited by migratory birds such as turnstone, oystercatcher and dunlin.

Other forms of wildlife found on the island include common lizard, slow worm and a rabbit population that has descended from ancestors introduced to the island for their skins and meat during the Middle Ages.

HOW TO GET THERE
Boat trips to Flat Holm are organised by the Flat Holm Project. Trips run from April and September and depart from Barry Docks. Advance booking is essential. For details contact the Flat Holm Project Office at Barry Docks (tel. 01446 747661) or visit their website: www.Cardiff.gov.uk/flatholm

ORDNANCE SURVEY MAPS
Landranger 1:50,000 series Nos. 171/182

TOURIST INFORMATION
Barry Tourist Information Centre, The Promenade, Barry CF62 5TQ (tel. 01446 747171) (seasonal) *or* Cardiff Visitor Centre, 16 Wood Street, Cardiff, CF10 1ER (tel. 029 2022 7281) Website: www.visitwales.com

WHERE TO STAY
Educational and working groups can stay on Flat Holm. For details contact the Flat Holm Project (see above). For accommodation in Barry contact the Tourist Information Centres in Barry (seasonal) or Cardiff.

ISLAND WALKS
A series of tracks and paths criss-cross the island. Visitors are accompanied by a warden and are requested not to wander from the prescribed routes.

PLACES TO VISIT
● Remains of cholera hospital (entry prohibited)
● Remains of Victorian and World War II gun emplacements
● Fog horn station
● Victorian barracks

Above *In 1737, after years of serious loss of life from shipwrecks in the treacherous waters of the Bristol Channel, a privately-funded lighthouse was built on Flat Holm. In 1820, the lighthouse was converted from a coal brazier to an oil-burning lamp. It was taken over by Trinity House in 1823, converted to electricity in 1969 and became automated in 1988. In the foreground is one of the abandoned Victorian 7-inch guns which can be seen scattered around the island.*

Index

Alderney *see* **Channel Islands**

Anglesey 126-133
Afon Cefni 131, 132
Agricola 127
Amlwch 126, 127, 129, 131
Amlwch Harbour 129, 131
Anglesey Sea Zoo 131
Barclodiad y Gawres 126
Beaumaris 126, 127, 128, 129
Beaumaris Castle 127
Black Death 129
Boudicca 127
Britannia Bridge 130, 132
Bryn Celli Ddu 126
Brynsiencyn 131
Bulkeley, Sir Richard 128
Cefni Reservoir 131
Chester & Holyhead Railway 130, 132
Cunedda 128
Din Lligwy 127
Dr Who 130
Edward I, King 127, 128
Gwynedd, Kingdom of 126, 128
Henry V, King 128
Henry VIII, King 128
Holy Island 129
Holyhead 129
James of St George 127
Llanfair PG 126, 133
Llangefni 132
Llyn Alaw Reservoir 130
Llyn Alaw wind farm 130
Llyn Cerrig Bach hoard 126
Malltraeth 131
Malltraeth Sands 131
Menai Bridge 124, 130, 132
Menai Strait 124, 126, 127, 129, 130, 131
Moelfre 127
National Grid 130
National Museum of Wales 126, 127
Newborough 127
Newborough Forest 131, 132
Newborough Warren 131
Owain Tudor 128
Parys Mountain 126, 127, 129, 130, 131
Penmon 128, 129
Penmon Cross 129
Plas Penmynydd 128
Priestholm Island 129
Puffin Island 128, 129
Red Wharf Bay 132
Rhosneigr 126
Rothesay Castle 128
Snowdonia 126
St Seiriol 128, 129
Stephenson, Robert 130
Telford, Thomas 124, 130, 132
Trywn Du lighthouse 128, 129
Tunnicliffe, Charles 132
Valley 126

Williams, Thomas 129
World War II 126
Wylfa Head 130
Wylfa nuclear power station 130

Bardsey Island 136-139
Aberdaron 138
Bardsey Apple 138
Bardsey Island Trust 136
Cowdray, Lord 136
Henry VIII, King 136
Lighthouse 139
Mynydd Enlli 136, 137, 138, 139
Newborough, Lord 136, 138
Porth Meudwy 138
Pwllheli 138
St Cadfan 136, 137
St Mary's Abbey 136, 137

Brownsea Island 64-67
Baden-Powell, Robert 65, 66
Benson, William 64
Bonham-Christie, Mary 65
Brownsea Castle 65
Cavendish-Bentinck, George 64
Cerne Abbey 64
Dorset Wildlife Trust 65, 66
Henry VIII, King 64
John Lewis Partnership 65
National Trust 64, 65
Poole Harbour 64, 65
pottery 67
Sturt, Sir Humphrey 64, 65
van Raalte, Charles 66
Waugh, Colonel William 64, 65

Bryher *see* **Scilly, Isles of**

Burgh Island 60-61
Avon, River 60
Bigbury Bay 60
Bigbury-on-Sea 60, 61
Chirgwin, Keith 60, 61
Christie, Agatha, 60
Coward, Noel, 60
Crocker, Tom 60
Dawson, Matthew 60
'Great White Palace' 60, 61
Johnson, Amy 60
Nettlefold, Archibald 60
Pilchard Inn 60, 61
Simpson, Wallis 61
South Hams 60
Wales, Prince of 61
World War II 61

Caldey Island 148-151
Bradshawe. John 148
Bushell, Rev W D
Caldey Abbey 148, 149
Caldey Stone 151
Carlyle, Benjamin 149
Fitzmartin, Robert 150
Henry I, King 148

Henry VIII, King 148
lighthouse 149
Nanna's Cave 148
Old Priory 148, 150
Prinknash Abbey 149
Priory Beach 148
Pyro 148
Red Berry Bay 150, 151
St Dogmael's 148
St Illtyd's church 151
St Margaret's Island 150
Tenby 148, 150
Trinity House 149

Canvey Island 88-91
Alfred, King 89
Arup, Sir Ove 89
Benfleet 89
Benfleet Creek 90, 91
Benfleet, Battle of 89
Brilleaux, Lee 89
Canvey Point 91
Dr Feelgood 89
Essex Wildlife Trust 90
Hadleigh Castle Country Park 90
Henry II, King 89
Hester, Frederick 90
Labworth Café 89
Leigh National Nature Reserve 90
Leigh on Sea 89
Lincolnshire 89
London 88, 89
Royal Society for the Protection of Birds 91
Shoebury 89
Sites of Special Scientific Interest 90
Southend-on-Sea 89
Thames estuary 89
Thames, River 89
Two Tree Island 90
West Canvey Marsh 91
Winter Garden 90
World War I 90
World War II 89, 90

Channel Islands 8-25
  Alderney 9, 22-25
    Alderney geranium 24
    Alderney Railway 25
    Alderney sea-lavender 24
    Alderney Wildlife Trust 24
    Braye Harbour 22, 23, 25
    Braye Road station 25
    British Admiralty 25
    Clonque Bay 22
    Fort Chateau a L'Etoc 22
    Henry VIII, King 22
    London Underground 25
    Longis Bay 22
    Mannez Quarry 23, 25
    Mont St Michel 22
    Normandy, Dukes of 22
    Quenard Point 9
    Saye Bay 22

St Anne 22
Weymouth 23
World War II 9, 22, 23

Guernsey 14-17
Castle Cornet 15
Cobo Bay 17
Duchy of Normandy 14
English Civil War 15
Fort Doyle 17
Fort Grey 16
Fort Hommet 17
Fort Saumarez 17
Great Western Railway 15
Guernsey Airport 16
Havelet Bay 14
Jerbourg Point 17
John, King 14, 15
L'Ancresse Bay 16
L'Ancresse Common 14
La Varde Dolmen 14
Le Grand Havre 17
Les Vauxbelets 17
Lihou Island 17
Little Chapel 17
Longsword, William 14
Martello towers 6, 15, 16
nature reserves 17
Normandy, Dukes of 14
Osborne, Sir Peter 15
Pembroke Bay 16
Pleinmont Point 16
Pope Sixtus IV 15
Portelet Harbour 17
Red Cross 16
Rocquaine Bay 16
Rollo 14
Shipwreck Museum 16
St Peter Port 14, 15, 16
St Sampson 14
Vazon Bay 17
Vega 16
Weymouth 16
William the Conqueror 14
World War II 16

Herm 18-19
Blücher von Wahlstatt, Prince 18
Blücher, Marshall 18
Common, The 19
Ford Motor Company 18, 19
Harbour, The 19
Jethou Island 19
Mackenzie, Compton 18, 19
Mont St Michel 18
Normandy, Dukes of 18
Perry, Sir Percival 18, 19
Rosaire Landing 19
Shell Beach 19
St Tugual
Waterloo, Battle of 18
White House Hotel 19
World War II 18

Jersey 10-13
Churchill, Winston 11
Corbière 11
Corbière lighthouse 12
de Rullecourt, Baron 11

Duchy of Normandy 10
Durrell Wildlife Conservation Trust 12
Durrell, Gerald 12
Elizabeth Castle 11
European Union 11
German Underground Hospital 13
Gorey 11
Green Lanes 13
Ho 8 13
Jersey Eastern Railway 11
Jersey Railway 11
John, King 11
La Cotte de St Brelade 10
La Hougue Bie 10
La Pulente 11, 13
La Rocco Tower 11
Les Minquiers 12
Martello towers 11
Mont Orgueil Castle 11
Normandy, Dukes of 10
Pinnacle Rock 10
Portelet 13
Queen's Valley 12
Ramsar Wetland Sites 12
Rozel 13
St Aubin 11, 13
St Aubin's Bay 10, 11
St Brelades 13
St Catherine's Wood 12
St Helier 10, 11
St Ouen's Bay 11, 12
St Ouen's Pond 12
St Peter's Valley 13
Vale de la Mare 12
William the Conqueror 10
World War II 11

Sark 20-21
Beaumont, Michael 21
Brecqhou Island 20
Carteret, Lord John 20
Chief Pleas 20
Creux Harbour 20
de Carteret, Helier 20
English Civil War 20
European Union 21
German Occupation 20
Gouliot Passage 20
Hathaway, Dame Sibyl 20, 21
Havre Gosselin 20
La Coupée 21
La Seigneurie 21
Masseline Harbour 20
Normandy, Dukes of 20
Sark Hoard 20
Sark prison 21
St Magloire 20
World War II 21

Farne Islands 104-107
Armstrong, Lord 105
Brownsman 105
Castell's Tower 104, 107
Convent of Durham 104
Darling, Grace 105, 107
Darling, William 105
Farne Islands Association 105
Forfarshire, SS 105

Henry VIII, King 104
House of Farne 104
Inner Farne 104, 105, 106, 107
Longstone lighthouse 105
National Trust 105
Seahouses 106
St Aidan 104
St Cuthbert 104
St Cuthbert's Chapel 104, 105, 107
Staple Island 104, 105, 106
Trinity House 105

Flat Holm 152-155
Bristol 152
Bristol Channel 152
Bute, Earls of 152
Cardiff 152, 153
Cardiff Corporation 152
Cardiff County Council 154
Cardiff Millennium Stadium 153
Flat Holm Project 154
fog horn 153
Glamorgan, Lords of 152
isolation hospital 153, 154
Lavernock Point 153
lighthouse 155
Marconi, Guglielmo 153
St Cadoc 152
Steep Holm 153
Trinity House 152, 155
World War II 152, 153

Foulness Island 92-93
Bennewith, John 92
Broomway, The 92
Churchend 93
Courtsend 92
Foulness Point 93
George & Dragon pub 92, 93
King's Head pub 92
Maplin Sands 92, 93
Ministry of Defence 92, 93
QinetiQ 92, 93
Samuel's Corner 92
Shrapnel, Henry 93
Site of Special Scientific Interest 93
Thames Estuary 93
War Department 92, 93

Guernsey *see* **Channel Islands**

Hayling Island 76-79
Black Death 76
Chichester Harbour 78
Domesday Book 76
East Hayling 77
East Hayling Light Railway 77
Funland Amusement Park 77
Hayling Billy Trail 78, 79
Jemièges, Abbey of 76
Langstone 76
Langstone Harbour 78, 79
Mulberry Harbours 78
Norfolk, Dukes of 76
Padwick, William 76
Portsmouth 78
Royal Hotel 77
Sandy Point Nature Reserve 78
Sinah Common 78

Solent, The 77, 78
South Hayling 77
South Hayling Manor 76
Station Theatre 78
World War II 78

Herm *see* **Channel Islands**

Holy Island 134-135
  Agricola 134
  Chester & Holyhead Railway 134,
    135
  Edward I, King 134
  Ellins Tower 135
  Heritage Coast 134, 135
  Holyhead 134
  Holyhead Mountain 134, 135
  Irish Mail 134
  London & North Western Railway
    134
  Porth Namarch 134
  Royal Society for the Protection of
    Birds 135
  South Stack 135
  South Stack lighthouse 135
  St Cybi 134
  St Cybi's church 135
  Stena Line 134
  Telford, Thomas 135
  Trearddur Bay 135

Holy Island (Lindisfarne) 108-111
  Bamburgh Castle 108
  Benedictine Priory, 111
  British Library 110
  Country Life 110
  Eadfrid of Lindisfarne, Bishop 110
  English Civil War 110
  English Heritage 111
  Henry VIII, King 108, 110, 111
  Hudson, Edward 110
  Iona 108
  Lindisfarne Castle 110
  Lindisfarne Gospels 109
  Links, The 111
  Lutyens, Sir Edwin 110
  National Trust 110
  Oswald of Northumbria, King 108
  Pilgrim's Way 109
  St Aidan 108
  St Cuthbert 108, 110
  St Mary's Church 110

Jersey *see* **Channel Islands**

Looe Island 58-59
  Atkins, Evelyn 59
  Cornwall Wildlife Trust 58, 59
  East Looe 58
  Glastonbury Abbey 58
  Jetty Cottage 58
  Looe Bay 58
  Marine Nature Reserve 58
  St George's Island 58
  Trelawny, Edward 58

Lundy Island 32-35
  Battery, The 35
  Christie, Augustus 33

Devil's Slide 35
Halfway Wall 34
Harman, Martin 33, 34
Hayward, Sir Jack 33
Heaven, Reverend Hudson 32
Heaven, William Hudson 32
Henry II, King 32
Landmark Trust 32, 33
Lundy cabbage 34
Lundy Field Society 34
Lundy ponies 34
marine nature reserve 33, 34
Mariscos 32
National Trust 32, 33, 34
North Light 34
Old Lighthouse 33
St Helena's Church 33
Trinity House 32, 33, 34

Man, Isle of 114-123
  Albert, Prince 114, 118
  Atholl, Duke of 119
  Ayres, The 120
  Ballaugh 121
  Calf of Man 121
  Calf Sound 121
  Castle Rushen 122
  Castletown 122
  Chasms 121
  Christian, William 119
  Close Sartfield 121
  Douglas 120, 1211
  Elizabeth I, Queen 122
  English Civil War 119
  Glen Rushen 121
  Godfred II, King 122
  Great Laxey Wheel 118
  Henry III, King 119
  Henry VI, King 119
  House of Keys 118, 120
  Isle of Man Forestry Department 122
  Isle of Man Railway 121
  Isle of Man TT races 114, 120
  Kingdom of Mann and the Isles 118
  'Lady Isabella' 118
  Laxey 118
  Legislative Council 118
  Liverpool 120
  Manx Bill of Rights 119
  Manx National Heritage 121
  Manx National Trust 121
  Manx Wildlife Trust 120, 122
  Marine Drive 123
  Maughold 117
  Maughold Head 120
  North Barrule 114
  Onchan 121
  Peel 115, 121
  Peel Castle 117
  Point of Ayre 114
  Port Erin 119, 121, 122, 123
  Port Soderick 123
  Ramsey 114, 116, 118, 119, 121
  Ramsey Bay 118
  Snaefell 119, 121
  South Barrule 117
  St German's cathedral 117
  St John's 118
  St Patrick's Isle 117

Stanley, Sir John 119
Stanley, Sir William 119
Sugarloaf 121
Sulby Reservoir 119
Tynwald 118. 119, 120
Tynwald Hill 118
Victoria, Queen 114, 118, 120

Mersea Island 98-101
  Brightlingsea 99, 101
  Colchester 98, 99
  Colchester Natural History Museum
    100, 101
  Colchester Oyster Festival 98
  Colne, River 98, 99, 101
  Cudmore Grove Country Park 100
  East Mersea 99
  English Civil War 98, 99
  Maldon, Battle of 99
  Mersea Seafood Festival 98
  Mersea Stone 99, 101
  oysters 98
  Point Clear 101
  Shepperton Studios 99
  Starfish Sites 99
  Strood, The 98
  Turner, Colonel Sir John 99
  West Mersea 86, 98, 99, 100
  West Mersea Yacht Club 98
  World War II 98, 99, 101

Northey Island 96-97
  Angell, Sir Norman 96
  Beeleigh Abbey 96
  Byrhtnoth, Earldorman 96
  Gate, Sir John 96
  Maldon 96
  Maldon, Battle of 96
  Mistley 97
  National Trust 96, 976
  River Blackwater 96
  Site of Special Scientific Interest 97
  South House Farm 96
  Thames sailing barges 97
  World War II 96

Ramsey Island 140-143
  Aber Mawr 142
  Bitches and Whelps 140
  Carn Llundain 140, 142
  Carn Ysgubor 140
  golden hair lichen 142
  Ramsey Sound 140
  Royal Society for the Protection of
    Birds 140, 141
  St David 140
  St David's 140
  St Justinian 142, 143
  Ynys Bery 141
  Ynys Cantwr 141

Sark *see* **Channel Islands**

Scilly, Isles of 36-55
  Bryher 50-51
    Anneka's Quay 51
    Blake, Admiral 50
    Church Quay 51
    English Civil War 50

Green Bay 50
Green, The 50
Hangman's Island 50
Heathy Hill 50, 51
Hell Bay Hotel 51
Minnehaha 50
Northern Rocks 51
Samson 50
Scilly Rock 50
Shipman Head Down 50
Works Point 50

St Agnes 42–45
Annet 42
Blanket Bay 44
Burnt Island 44
Camper Dizzle Point 45
Castle Vean 44
Cornwall, Duchy of 43
Firebrand, HMS 43
Gugh 43
Isles of Scilly Wildlife Trust 43
lighthouse 43
Lower Town 44, 45
Periglis Bay 45
Shovell, Admiral Sir Cloudsley 43
Smith Sound 43
St Warna's Well 43
Troy Town maze 45
Wingletang Down 43

St Martin's 52–55
Arthur 54
Blake, Admiral 53
Chapel Down 52, 53
Cornwall, Duchy of 53
Cruther's Hill 52
Day Mark 52, 53
Eastern Isles 55
Ganilly 54
Higher Town 55
Higher Town Bay 55
Higher Town Quay 55
Lower Town Quay 55
Men-a-vaur 54
Nornour 52, 54
Round Island 54
Smith, Augustus 53
St Elidius 54
St Helen's 54
St Martin's Bay 53
St Martin's Hotel 54
St Theona 52
Tean 52
Wesley, John 53

St Mary's 42–45
Church Point 38
Cornwall, Duchy of 38, 39
Elizabeth I, Queen 38
Falmouth 39
Garrison, The 36, 39, 40, 41
Giant's Tomb 38
Godolphin, Francis 38, 39
Halangy Down 38, 40
Harry's Walls 38
Henry I, King 38
Hugh Town 38, 39, 40
Innisidgen 38

kelp pits 39
Mount Flagon 38
Nature reserves 41
Old Town Bay 41
Peninnis Head 40, 41
Porth Hellick 38
Scillonian III 39, 40
Smith, Augustus 39
Star Castle 38, 39, 41
Tavistock Abbey 38
Toll's Island 39

Tresco 46–49
Abbey Pool 48
Bathinghouse Porth 46
Benedictine priory 46
Blake, Admiral 46, 48
Cornwall, Duchy of 46, 47
Cromwell's Castle 46, 48
Dorrien-Smith 46, 47, 48
English Civil War 46, 48
Ennor 46
Farm Beach 48
Great Pool 48
Henry I, King 46
Island Hotel 49
New Grimsby 46, 49
New Grimsby 47
New Grimsby Harbour 46, 48
New Inn 49
Old Grimsby 46
Oliver's Battery 46
Pentle Bay 46
Smith, Augustus 46, 47, 48
Tavistock Abbey 46
Tregarthen Hill 46
Tresco Abbey 47, 48
Tresco Abbey Gardens 46, 47, 48, 49

St Agnes *see* **Scilly, Isles of**

St Martin's *see* **Scilly, Isles of**

St Mary's *see* **Scillyy, Isles of**

Sheppey, Isle of 82–85
Aethelberht, King 82
Charles II, King 83
Eastchurch 84
Edward III, King 83
Elmley Marshes 84
Faversham 84
Ferry Inn 82, 85
Flushing 84
Harty Ferry 84
Harty Marshes 82
Harty, Isle of 84
Her Majesty's Prisons 84
James II, King 84
King's Ferry 84
Kingsferry Bridge 83
Leysdown-on-Sea 84
London Chatham & Dover Railway 84
Medway Estuary 82, 83, 84
Pepys, Samuel 83
Pugin, E W 85
Queenborough 83, 84
Richard Montgomery, SS 82

Rolls, Charles 84
Royal Society for the Protection of Birds 84
Seaxburga, Queen 82
Sheerness 84, 85
Shell Ness 85
Sheppey Crossing 83
Short Brothers 84
Swale National Nature Reserve 84
Swale, The 82, 83, 84
Thames Estuary 83
William of Orange 84

Skomer Island 144–147
European Marine Site 146
Grassholm 146
Jack Sound 144
Kensington, Lord 144
Lockley, Ronald 147
Martin's Haven 146
Neale, J J 144
Neck, The 144
Philipps, William 147
Skokholm Island 147
West Wales Field Society 144
Wick, The 145
Wildlife Trust of South and West Wales 145, 147
World War II 144

St Michael's Mount 56–57
Arundell, Sir Humphrey 56
Basset, Francis 56
Cecil, Sir Robert 56
de la Pomeray, Henry 56
Henry VI, King 56
Marazion 57
Mont St Michel 56
Mortain, Count of 56
Mount's Bay 56, 57
National Trust 56, 57
Oxford, Earl of 56
Salisbury, Earl of 56
Spanish Armada 57
St Aubyn, John 56
St Aubyn, Piers 57
St Levan, Lord 57
Syon Abbey 56
underground railway 57
Warbeck, Perkin 56
Warspite, HMS 57
William the Conqueror 56

Steep Holm 28–31
Allsop, Kenneth 29
Augustinian priory
Banks, Sir Joseph 30
Berkeley Castle 28
Berkeley, Lords of 28, 30
Bristol Channel 28, 29, 30
Kenneth Allsop Memorial Trust 28, 29, 30
Rudder Rock 28
Split Rock Battery 31
St Gildas 28
Steep Holm Peony 30
Steep Holm Trust 30
Uphill Manor, Lord of 28
World War I 29

World War II 28, 29, 30, 31

Thorney Island 80-81
Baker Barracks 80
Chichester Harbour 80, 81
Coastal Command 80, 81
Domesday Book 80
Great Deep 80
Little Deep 80
Ministry of Defence 80, 81
Osbern, Bishop 80
Royal Air Force 80
St Nicholas Church 80
Warlewaste, Bishop 80
West Thorney 80
World War II 80

Tresco *see* **Scilly, Isles of**

Wallasea Island 94-95
Burnham-on-Crouch 95
Creeksea Ferry Inn 94, 95
Essex Marina 94, 95
Essex Wildlife Trust 95
Lion Creek Nature Reserve 94
Paglesham Creek 95
River Crouch 95
Wallasea Wetlands Project 94
World War II 95

Walney, Isle of 112-113
Awdry, Rev W 112
Barrow-in-Furness 112, 113
Cumbria Wildlife Trust 113
English Civil War 112, 113
Furness Abbey 112, 113
Isle of Walney Estates Company 112
Jubilee Bridge 112
North Scale 112
North Walney 112
North Walney Reserve 113

Piel Island 112, 113
Piel, King of 113
R80 113
Roa Island 113
South Walney Reserve 113
Thomas the Tank Engine 112
U21 113
Vickers 112
Vickerstown 112, 113
Walney Channel 112
Wordsworth, William 113
World War I 113
World War II 113

Wight, Isle of 68-75
Albert, Prince 73
Appuldurcombe House 73
Bembridge 72
Bembridge Harbour 74
Black Arrow 71
Black Knight 69, 71
Brading 68
Brading Marshes 72
Brightstone Bay 72
Britten-Norman 72
Brook Bay 72
Brown, Capability 73
Caedwalla, King 68
Carisbrooke Castle 69
Charles I, King 69
Compton Bay 71, 72
Cowes 69, 70, 72
Cowes Week 72
Culver Cliff 75
de Redvers, Richard, 69
East Cowes 72
English Heritage 73
Fitz-Osbern, William 69
Freshwater 68
Freshwater Bay 71
Haven Street 74

Henry VIII, King 69
Isle of Wight Coastal Path 74, 75
Isle of Wight Festival 72
Isle of Wight Steam Railway 74
Mottistone 68
National Trust 68, 72
Needles Battery 70
Needles, The 69, 72
Newport 68
Newtown Harbour Nature Reserve 72
Osborne House 70, 73
PLUTO 72
Portsmouth 70
Princess flying boat 72
Ryde 70
Ryde Esplanade 73
Ryde Pier 73
Sandown 69, 75
Saunders, S E 72
Saunders-Roe 71
Shanklin 70, 72
Sites of Special Scientific Interest 72
Smallbrook Junction 74
Solent, The 70
Spanish Armada 69
Spithead 70
Swiss Cottage 73
Tennyson Down 62, 68, 71, 72
Tennyson, Alfred, Lord 62, 68
Vectis 68
Ventnor 70
Victoria, Queen 70, 73
Westover Down 68
White, J Samuel 72
William the Conqueror 69
Wootton 74
World War I 72
World War II 71, 73
Worsley, Richard 69
Wroxall 73
Yarmouth 69

AUTHOR'S ACKNOWLEDGEMENTS

I would like to thank the many people who have made the production of this book possible: to the publishers, Frances Lincoln, and in particular to John Nicholl; for technical support Chas Stoddard, David Titchener and Nigel White; to the editor, Denise Stobie, for her unfailing enthusiasm and to the proofreader, Linda Wright; to the many helpful tourist information centres for arranging my accommodation; to the boatmen and helicopter pilots who carried me safely to my destinations; to the English and Welsh weather for behaving itself; to the many islanders who I met on my travels; to Francis Laver for his excellent company and last, but not least, to my wife, Sarah, for her unfailing support and assistance during the making of this book.